WECK®

Home Preserving

WECK®

Home Preserving

Made-from-Scratch Recipes for Water-Bath Canning, Fermenting, Pickling, and More

STEPHANIE THUROW
Master Food Preserver

Skyhorse Publishing

Copyright © 2020 by Stephanie Thurow
Photography © 2020 by Stephanie Thurow

Skyhorse Publishing books may be purchased in bulk at special discounts for sales promotion, corporate gifts, fund-raising, or educational purposes. Special editions can also be created to specifications. For details, contact the Special Sales Department, Skyhorse Publishing, 307 West 36th Street, 11th Floor, New York, NY 10018 or info@skyhorsepublishing.com.

Skyhorse® and Skyhorse Publishing® are registered trademarks of Skyhorse Publishing, Inc.®, a Delaware corporation.

Visit our website at www.skyhorsepublishing.com.

10 9 8 7 6 5 4 3 2

Library of Congress Cataloging-in-Publication Data is available on file.

Cover design by Daniel Brount
Cover photo by Stephanie Thurow

Print ISBN: 978-1-5107-5127-9
Ebook ISBN: 978-1-5107-5129-3

Printed in China

Dedicated to my Sophia

CONTENTS

INTRODUCTION

I'm pleased to bring you another flavor-packed preserving guide designed specifically for WECK jars. In this book you will find explanations for how to water-bath can and ferment from the comfort of your home. Some recipes are written for water-bath canning to create shelf-stable pantry preserves, others are all about how to ferment fruits and vegetables into healthy probiotic-rich ferments through wild fermentation (no starter cultures required), and remaining are some of my favorite made-from-scratch recipes (that are not water-bath canned or fermented). All can be stored in gorgeous WECK jars.

My affinity for WECK jars began over a decade ago. That's when I slowly began collecting them, one style at a time. I enjoy using WECK jars because they are aesthetically pleasing, and I like using the different styles for different preserves. However, my favorite part about these jars is that they are glass and reusable. Less waste and no funny chemicals are leaching into my homemade preserves. Being such a superfan of the jars, you can only imagine my excitement when the J. Weck Company chose to collaborate with me on not only one, but two cookbooks!

As with all my cookbooks, the recipes are written in an easy-to-understand format and yield only a small batch. Small-batch recipes are great because it means less prep time, less expense for the ingredients, and less storage space required. Plus, it's a fantastic way to test out a recipe without investing too much time, money, or energy.

There are numerous note boxes throughout this cookbook. I find this to be a useful workspace for noting likes, dislikes, and changes made to recipes. I encourage you to use my recipes as a jumping-off point for your preservation creations. Enjoy!

Stephanie

PART I

THE HISTORY OF WECK® JARS

A chemist named Dr. Rudolf Rempel discovered that food could be successfully preserved by heating it in glass jars with an abraded edge, rubber ring, and metal lid. His discovery was patented in 1892, but he died in 1893. Albert Hussener founded a company that produced glass jars, but the company was not successful, probably because of the lack of advertising for his new product. He sold the patent to Johann Weck.

Johann Weck was born near Frankfurt, Germany. He moved to the town of Öflingen, in the state of Baden, as soon as he had bought Rempel's patent. Weck was a strict vegetarian and an abstainer from alcohol. With his products he wanted to fight against the disease of alcoholism which was very common at the time. The surroundings in southern Baden were rich in fruit trees and fulfilled his wishes of preserving fruit instead of using it to make alcohol. He had acquired the exclusive right for distribution of the newly patented glass jars and canning apparatus for the entire area of southern Germany. He also bought the sole proprietorship of the company and the WECK canning patent.

He realized very soon that he could not manage the whole project alone. He found a partner from the Lower Rhine area who was the local sales distributor for WECK products. The businessman, Georg van Eyck, was operating a porcelain and pottery shop. Around 1895, he took up the offer of Joann Weck to sell home canning jars. Georg van Eyck sold more canning jars in his shop alone than were sold in all other shops in Germany. Van Eyck had a special commercial talent, and he realized that he had to introduce his customers to the practical side of food preservation. When Weck asked him how he succeeded in selling so many jars, he also asked him if he would come to Öflingen to take over the sales of WECK products for all of Germany. Van Eyck agreed and founded together with Johann Weck the J. Weck Company on January 1, 1900.

With foresight and energy Georg van Eyck built up the company in Germany and the neighboring countries of Austria, Belgium, France, Hungary, Luxembourg, the Netherlands, and Switzerland. He did not become discouraged when Johann Weck decided to leave the firm in 1902 for personal reasons. Van Eyck built up his own staff and organized introductory sales shows for the whole country, just as he had done at his own shop. He employed teachers of domestic science who gave practical advice and instructions at cooking classes, parishes, and hospitals. He constantly improved his products: the jars, rubber sealing, canners, thermometers, and all the accessories, which were sold under the trademark of WECK. With the trademark WECK, Georg van Eyck created one of the first trademarks in Germany, and also used advanced strategies of advertising by introducing the trademark name written across a red strawberry, which is still a well-known German label today.

Both world wars resulted in big setbacks for the WECK Company. When World War I started, all foreign trade contracts with the European countries and Russia came to a halt. In World War II, the three WECK glass factories that were located in the East were confiscated without damages being paid.

The WECK glass factory near Bonn—still under the ownership of the grandchildren of its founder Georg van Eyck—took up production after the war, in 1950. It has developed into a very modern, almost fully automated glass factory which today produces not only home canning jars but also bottles for soft drinks, jars and commercially preserved foods. The WECK Company has also produced a home and garden magazine *Ratgeber Frau und Familie* ("Advisor—Woman and Family") for more than 117 years. This monthly magazine is read in more than one million German-speaking households. The headquarters of the J. WECK Company are still in Öflingen, Germany.

ABOUT WECK® JARS

WECK jars are gorgeous tempered-glass jars and come in a variety of shapes and sizes. Each jar has a distinctive orange rubber ring, a glass lid, and two rustproof stainless-steel clamps that securely close the jar. The metal clamps fit all WECK jars, and the jar lids and rubber rings of different styles fit interchangeably on jars of the same size.

Cylindrical jars are ideal for both canning and fermenting. The tall, thin design of jar model numbers 905 and 908 make them perfect for asparagus pickles (pg. 73). The smaller cylindrical jars (905) are great for infusions (pgs. 127, 129, and 131), and the larger jars (908 and 974) are fantastic for ferments such as sauerkraut (pg. 90).

Deco jars are beautifully shaped and ideal for canning jams and sauces, and for storing flavored salts (pg. 121) and sugars (pg. 125). Due to their shape, they are not recommended for whole fruit or whole vegetable water-bath canning. They are also great for decorative purposes and dried food storage.

Deli jars are also ideal for flavored salts and sugars, or dried food/seasoning storage. This style is also great for pourable preserves, such as infused honey (pg. 127), syrup (pg. 129) and vinegar (pg. 131).

Juice jars of all sizes are wonderful jars to use for pourable infusions. The neck of the jar helps keep the infused ingredients submerged.

Mini mold jars are so adorable. It's surprising all the ways you'll find to fill them. I use the smallest of the collection (080 and 756) for organizing salts, sugars, and dried seasonings, and also for single servings of canned ketchup (pg. 59).

Mold jars are the most common style of jars used in my home, next to the cylindrical jars. They are perfect for both ferments and canned goods, and are preferred to freeze with! These jars in their various sizes are great for pickles, jams, preserved lemons (pg. 139) and pretty much everything.

Tulip jars are shapely and gorgeous once filled. The smallest two of the collection (762 and 746) are perfect for jams and chutneys. The 745 jar is closest to a quart and excellent for canning pickles and fermenting.

Keep Fresh Covers come in small, medium, large, and extra-large. The BPA-free, reusable, dishwasher-safe lids are convenient for closing a lid on an open preserve or for freezing with the Mold-style jars. The varying cover sizes fit on a wide assortment of WECK jars.

WECK jars are European and therefore do not translate exactly to American sizing of half pint, pint, and quart. However, they have jars very similar in size. Here is a list of the styles of jars that I most commonly use for canning and fermenting that are most similar to an 8–fl. ounce jam jar, a 16–fl. ounce pint jar, and a 32–fl. ounce quart jar.

WECK® jars closest to an 8 fl. oz. jam jar

Jar Style	Style #	Size (Liters)	Fluid Ounces
Deco Jar	902	⅕ L	7.4 fl. oz.
Mold Jar	740	⅕ L	9.8 fl. oz.
Mold Jar	900 (tall)	⅕ L	9.8 fl. oz.
Tulip	762	⅕ L	7.4 fl. oz.

WECK® jars closest to a 16 fl. oz. pint jar

Jar Style	Style #	Size (Liters)	Fluid Ounces
Deco Jar	901	½ L	18.9 fl. oz.
Mold Jar	741	¼ L	12.5 fl. oz.
Mold Jar	742	½ L	19.6 fl. oz.
Tulip Jar	744	½ L	19.6 fl. oz.

WECK® jars closest to a 32 fl. oz. quart jar

Jar Style	Style #	Size (Liters)	Fluid Ounces
Cylindrical Jar	908	1 L	35.2 fl. oz.
Deco Jar	748	1 L	35.9 fl. oz.
Mold Jar	743	¾ L	28.7 fl. oz.
Tulip Jar	745	1 L	35.9 fl. oz.

WECK jars have not been tested by the USDA for home canning, therefore are not "approved" by the USDA for home canning, but this does not mean they are not safe for home canning. They have been safely used in home and commercial canning in Europe and around the world since 1900. The recipes in this book have been designed for WECK jars specifically, though measurements can be converted to fit standard 8-ounce, 16-ounce, and 32-ounce home canning jars that are USDA-approved. Please keep in mind that the headspace recommended per recipe will vary from ½ to ¼ inches if using any jar other than a WECK jar. Water-bath canned recipes from other cookbooks can be converted to fit WECK jars in a relatively similar size by adjusting the headspace to ½ inch.

CANNING AND FERMENTING: EXPLAINING THE DIFFERENCES

If you've read either of my other books, *Can It & Ferment It* or *WECK Small-Batch Preserving*, parts of the next few sections may be a bit of a repeat, though I encourage you to keep reading as bits and pieces vary and are tailored to WECK jars.

Water-Bath Canning

The process of water-bath canning allows us to preserve food with freshness and at peak flavor. This method of preservation creates an airtight environment in which bacteria and other harmful contaminates cannot survive after going through the high-heat process of the boiling water bath. Through this preservation process, acidic canned goods become shelf-stable and can be stored in a pantry or cupboard for one to two years. They can keep for more than one year, but for the best flavor, texture, nutrients, and taste, try to keep to the 12- to 18-month time frame, as it all begins to deplete once preserved.

Fermenting

Fermented recipes in this book are fruits or vegetables that are fermented with salt or in a saltwater brine (salt dissolved in water). The process of fermentation can take days, weeks, months, or even years depending on the flavor desired and the specific fruit or vegetable used (though the recipes in this book generally take only a few days or weeks to ferment). The process of lactic acid fermentation creates an acidic environment (lactobacillus converts sugar into lactic acid) where bad/unsafe bacteria cannot survive and good bacteria (probiotics) can thrive. This process is also known as "lacto-fermentation" or "wild fermentation." Lactic acid preserves the texture, taste, and nutrients in fermented foods. Fermented produce contains plentiful and varied probiotics, which are beneficial to your digestive system. The studies on fermented foods are endless and truly fascinating to read. If you haven't already, I encourage you to take some time to research the topic and the health benefits linked to fermented foods. Much research is being done in the field of fermented foods, and, as the scientists learn more, they are finding how beneficial fermented foods truly are to our bodies and minds. See the resources section in the back of the book for reading recommendations (pg. 150).

Importance of Local and Organic Produce in Canned and Fermented Foods

Always preserve with the freshest available fruits and vegetables whenever possible; they are going to have the best flavor if they are picked at their peak and also retain more nutritional value compared to produce from the grocery store. Most of the produce sold at the grocery store is picked long before it's ripe, and, by the time it reaches the store shelves, it has lost many of its vitamins and nutrients. Per the USDA National Institute of Food and Agriculture, produce that is canned promptly after harvest can be more nutritious than fresh produce sold in local stores. The

USDA goes on to say that within one to two weeks, even refrigerated produce loses half or more of some of its vitamins. I recommended buying produce at the farmers' market that has been harvested the day of or the day prior, that way the produce is preserved within 24 to 48 hours of when it's harvested. Use organic produce whenever possible and always use produce that is not treated with a food-grade wax sealant or harsh chemicals. *Wash all produce thoroughly before using.*

In addition to using freshly harvested foods, when selecting produce be sure to pick fruits and vegetables that are not bruised or damaged. For some recipes it is beneficial to try and select produce that's uniform in size (an example would be when making pickles). Having uniformity allows the produce to pickle evenly, which will result in a consistent end product.

Farmers are happy to explain their farming practices, and I have found that many fruits and vegetables are indeed farmed organically, but the farmers have not gone through the process of making that official due to the cost incurred. Do not hesitate to ask the farmers questions about their farming practices, because you might be pleasantly surprised by their answers. Be sure to always ask when the produce was harvested to ensure freshness.

CANNING INGREDIENTS AND SUPPLIES

Salt (for Water-Bath Canning): Canning salt, also known as "pickling salt," is preferred; it is pure sodium chloride. Kosher salt is also acceptable, though the amounts may vary. Be sure to check a salt conversion chart. You can find one at: www.mortonsalt.com/article/salt-conversion-chart/. Never use iodized salt.

Vinegar: Only use vinegars that indicate a 5–6 percent acidity level. Many bottles will note "pickling vinegar" on the packaging. I've personally only used store-bought vinegar because it offers reliable acidity results and I know it's safe. For the sake of simplicity, every water-bath canned recipe in this cookbook will call for 5 percent acidity, distilled white vinegar, or organic apple cider vinegar.

Sugar: As you've probably noticed, canned jams, jellies, chutneys, and other sweet preserves generally include more granulated sugar than you'd expect. Sugar helps not only preserve the color, but also helps the canned goods gel and become firm instead of syrup-like. Ohio State University Extension Services states that sugar also acts as a preservative by inhibiting microbial activity; thus, recipes should not be modified or adapted. Brown sugar and honey can be substituted for granulated sugar in recipes, though it will not cut down the overall carbohydrate content. It is not promoted by the Extension Services to use artificial sweeteners when canning preserves. However, there are liquid and powder pectin options on the market that will help reduce sugar in recipes, though none of the recipes in this book call for them. If you purchase pectin to reduce sugar in these recipes, please be sure to read the directions that come with the pectin packaging to fully understand how to use it. Pectin can be found online or in the canning section of most supermarkets.

Water: The purest water you have available to you is the best option. I have a reverse osmosis system at home that I often use. Water with minerals such as iron could cause discoloration but is fine to use. I've canned with tap water for many years, and it's worked great with the water from the city where I live. Some chemicals added to city water could possibly cause an adverse reaction to the end product, but you may need to learn by trial and error to know if your tap water will work. If you are in a rural area and have well water as your main source, you can have the water tested to see if there has been any contamination. If you are unsure, store-bought water is an option.

Lemon Juice: A couple of recipes in this book call for lemon juice. Use fresh juice from lemons or store-bought lemon juice, but know that it is recommended by the USDA to use store-bought lemon juice when canning, since the acidity level is reliable when compared to using fresh lemons.

Common Canning Supplies

- Large water bath–canning pot with lid and a rack, 21–33 quarts in size. These are typically sold in big-box stores in a starter set or online. The rack is required to keep the jars off the bottom of the pot and allows water to flow around all sides of the jars. Canning pots range from about $20 to $100. Read the range recommendations for each water-bath canner; some do not work with electric, glass-top ranges. If canning one single jar, a fourth burner pot comes in handy as it comes with a rack to hold your jar off the bottom and heats quickly. Two small jars can be canned at the same time with a fourth burner pot, but there must be a barrier between the jars. These pots usually range between $30 and $50.

- Stainless-steel regular-mouth funnel.
- WECK jars in a variety of sizes and styles, including the rubber rings and metal clamps they come with.
- WECK jar lifter to insert and remove jars from the hot water bath. WECK offers a specialized jar lifter that works well with the unique shapes of their jars.
- Stainless-steel potato masher, used when making jam.
- Stainless-steel ladle.
- Measuring cups in a variety of sizes.
- Measuring spoons in a variety of sizes.
- Clean lint-free towels or paper towels.
- Sharp paring knife.
- Stainless-steel butter knife, used to remove air pockets from hot and cold packed jars.
- Large- and medium-sized thick bottomed, nonreactive (stainless-steel or enamel-lined) pots for making jams, sauces, and brines.
- Candy thermometer, to measure the temperature of the water or jam sauce (not required for any of the recipes in this book, but convenient to have on hand if you want to test jam or water temperature).
- Occasionally throughout the book, a food processor, fine mesh strainer, mandolin slicer, apple peeler, or hand blender would streamline the process in some recipes. These are not required for canning but are very helpful to have on hand when needed.

The USDA recommends using plastic utensils when canning; however, I personally only use stainless steel, as I do not like to heat plastic. I've never had a jar break due to using stainless steel, but if you are leery, feel free to use plastic funnels, ladles, and other utensils.

CANNING WITH WECK®

Food Safety Recommendations

Jars filled with raw-packed food must be processed in warmer water and slowly heated to a rolling boil, to allow the contents to gradually heat up to avoid jar breakage. Make sure the water-bath canner is hot but not simmering, then submerge all jars in the water bath, cover the water-bath pot with the lid, and increase temperature so the contents of the jar can safely heat to a rolling boil. Once the canner has reached a boil, start the timer per your recipe instructions.

Due to food safety recommendations in America, the orange rubber rings on WECK jars should be replaced after each water bath, though in Europe (where the jars have been used for home canning for more than one hundred years) the rubber rings are reused multiple times until they stretch, crack, or break. I've been canning with WECK jars for more than a decade, and I've always reused the rings without a problem. However, if the rubber ring is cracked, overstretched, or broken, do not use it for home canning. To inspect rubber rings for flaws before processing, hold the ring between your thumb and forefinger with both hands and tug lightly while turning the ring clockwise. WECK rubber rings are perfectly safe to reuse over and over for fermentation, but use your judgment when deciding whether to replace or reuse the ring each time it's used for water-bath canning.

Hot Pack versus Cold Pack

There are two main ways to fill jars when canning. The hot pack method is when a jar is filled with hot, precooked food such as jam. The cold pack a.k.a. raw pack method is when a jar is filled with uncooked produce and the fruit or veggies are covered with a hot liquid brine or syrup. The liquid needs to be hot during this process; otherwise, there is a risk of the jar breaking during the water-bath process. A jar breaking during processing will occasionally happen (even to the best of us) and unfortunately all contents of the broken or cracked jar must be carefully disposed of and cannot be reused. Both methods of hot and cold packing result in sealing the jars via the boiling hot water-bath method. It's important to always leave headspace in the jars between the top of the liquid or food and rim of the jar. When canning with other jars, the recipes vary from ¼ to ½ inches of headspace for water-bath canned recipes, but because this cookbook is designed for WECK jars, all water-bath canned recipes will require the same ½ inch of headspace per the WECK Company's recommendation. This extra space allows for expansion of the food in the jar during the sealing process. When packing jars with fruits or veggies in preparation for the hot water bath, it's important to try and remove any air bubbles trapped within the contents of the jar to reduce the risk of spoilage. I use a stainless-steel chopstick to aid in removing bubbles when packing hot and cold packs, but a stainless-steel butter knife works just as well.

The Process of Boiling

Water-bath canning involves submerging filled jars into a hot water bath. This process kills bacteria that might otherwise cause spoilage and creates a vacuum that removes air from jars and seals them tightly to prevent any outside contamination. This process allows for long-term storage without refrigeration.

When canning, always be sure to check the rims of the jars and lids to make sure there are no cracks or chips. Do not use jars with defects or they will not properly seal. Per the USDA, jars filled with high-acid preserves that are water-bath canned ten minutes or longer do not require sterilization. Every canning recipe in this book will be processed ten minutes or longer, but I urge you to wash all canning jars with hot water and soap and rinse thoroughly before use. I use a dishwasher to clean my jars, rings, and lids at the same time and I leave them in the dishwasher so they keep warm until I'm ready to fill them.

If you do not have a dishwasher, heat your jars after washing them to keep them warm before filling them. The National Center for Home Preservation recommends submerging jars in hot water, right-side up in the water-bath canner, with water one inch above the jars. Turn the heat up once submerged and allow the jars to simmer until you are ready to fill them with food. Use a jar lifter to carefully remove the jars from the water, cautiously dump out the hot water back into the water-bath canner, and carefully set the jars on a clean towel and allow them to cool slightly. Use a small to medium saucepan (depending on lid/ring size you are using) to gently simmer the WECK lids and rubber rings until they are ready to be used, then set them out on a clean towel or napkin for quick access right before use. Jars need to remain warm until they are ready to be filled. Doing so will help avoid breakage of the jars from what is called "thermal shock," which can occur when there is a drastic temperature difference.

Fill water-bath canner with water and bring to a boil. This water will never touch the contents of your preserves. Starting the water-bath canner is one of the first steps I take when canning because it can take a long time for it to reach a boil. The size of jars being sealed will determine how much water to add to the canning pot. If using small jars, the pot only needs to be filled up about halfway (depending on the height of the rack). Keep in mind that once the jars are added to the pot, the water line will rise. You want the water to cover the submerged jars by about one inch when you begin the boiling-water-bath processing time.

Once you're ready to fill jars with fruit/veggies always leave ½ inch of headspace, use a stainless-steel butter knife or other nonreactive tool to remove any air bubbles trapped within the produce and jar (if needed). Next, use a slightly dampened lint-free towel or paper towel to clean the rim of the jar. Remove any traces of food or liquid and wipe again with a dry paper towel to clean the lip of the jar. Place the orange rubber ring and lid on the jar and clip the metal clamps on directly across from one another. The jar and its contents will be hot, so you may need to grip the jar with a towel when adding the metal clamps so you do not burn yourself. It is recommended to read the instructions that come with WECK jars if you have never canned before. Once the water bath is ready, use the jar lifter to carefully transfer the jars into the hot water bath; make sure to keep the jars level.

Sea level plays a factor in how long jars will boil in the water bath. All recipes in this book are based on processing at an elevation of 1,000 feet above sea level or below. See chart and add time to each recipe as needed.

Sea Level	Processing Time
1,001–3,000 ft.	Add 5 minutes to the processing time
3,001–6,000 ft.	Add 10 minutes to the processing time
6,001+ ft.	Add 15 minutes to the processing time

Once the processing time ends, turn the heat to low and let the boiling water settle down for a minute or two. Then, use the jar lifter to carefully lift the jars out of the hot water bath and transfer the jars to a towel-covered counter or table where they will not be disturbed for 12 or more hours. After 12 hours, remove the metal clamps from the jars and test each jar to make sure it is sealed. To test the seal of the jar, simply try to remove the lid from the jar. If it easily lifts off, it has not sealed. The lid should be securely suctioned to the jar to have a successful seal. If a jar does not seal after 12 hours, you can keep it in the refrigerator and use within a couple of weeks.

Store sealed canned goods in a dark, dry, and cool place. Keep the metal clamps off the canned goods while in storage to prevent jars from breaking on the rare instance that something begins to spoil if it did not seal properly. If the clamps are removed from the sealed jar, the lid will pop off if something spoils, versus a possible jar break from pressure buildup, and creating a mess. For this same reason, it is not recommended to stack your canned goods either. We have an old well in our home that's been covered and the previous owners built shelves on the walls to store canned goods on. It's the perfect spot to keep the sealed preserves; organized, dark, and cool. If you don't have a basement or a space like this, put them on the bottom shelf of a cupboard. Refrain from storing the jars up high, as heat rises. According to the USDA, it is best to store your goods between 50° and 70°F (10 and 21°C). You do not want to display them in a location where they get direct sunlight. Sunlight can cause the color of your preserve to change as well as the texture and flavor, and it can also deplete nutrients from the canned good.

Refrigerate all canned goods after breaking the seal. Fruit-based preserves will last about two months after opening and vinegar-based preserves are best consumed within six months.

But what about the B-word? Botulism. Botulism is a life-threatening disease that is caused by ingesting the clostridium botulinum bacteria. The bacteria grows in low-oxygen environments; however, it cannot grow below a pH of 4.6. Acidic foods, or foods that have been acidified (like pickles, for example) can safely be preserved by following safe, trusted recipes. Each water-bath canned recipe throughout this book has a pH below 4.6, and therefore is safe for home canning. Foods with a pH above 4.6 that are not acidified will need to be canned with a pressure cooker in order to reach high enough temperatures to destroy the C. botulinum spores.

Each recipe in this book has a estimated yield amount. The amount per recipe can vary due to the size of fruits or vegetables used. I recommend preparing one or two extra jars in case a recipe makes more than the suggested yield amount. Jars not full enough to be water-bath sealed can be cooled and stored in the refrigerator in an airtight container, but because the preserve did not go through the process of food sterilization from the boiling water bath, it will not last as long in the fridge and will need to be eaten within a couple of weeks (fruit-based preserves) or months (pickles).

CANNING WITH WECK® STEP-BY-STEP

Before canning with WECK jars, inspect the lids and jars for cracks or chips. Should the sealing rim of a jar or sealing portion of the lid be chipped/damaged, recycle it as it will not permit an airtight seal, or reserve it for fermentation use only. All jars should be cleaned with hot, soapy water or run through the dishwasher before use.

1.

Keep jars, lids, and rings warm in either the dishwasher or warm water until use. When ready to can, carefully empty hot water from jars or take a warm jar straight from the dishwasher.

2b.

Fill jars, leaving ½ inch of headspace.

2a.

Use a funnel to safely transfer the hot brine/preserve into each jar.

3.

Wipe the rim of the jar with a clean, dampened, lint-free cloth or paper towel, then again with a dry towel.

4.

Place the rubber ring on the lid. Place the lid with ring on the rim of the jar.

5.

Use the two metal clamps to secure the lid on the jar. Using two hands, carefully hook the clamp on the top lid of the jar first, then press firmly until it clicks under the rim of the jar. Still holding the jar, clip the other clamp on directly across from the other. Use a towel if needed to hold jar in place while clipping on the clamps so you do not burn your fingers if the jar contents are hot.

6.

Use the jar lifter to carefully place jars on the canning pot rack, in the hot water bath. Jars should be completely submerged in water by at least 1 inch. The temperature of the water bath should be similar to the temperature of the canned food you are submerging in the water to avoid breakage. WECK jars can touch one another and/or the canning pot wall of the water bath canner while processing, however they should not be tipped or wedged in the pot. You can stack WECK jars during the water bath–canning process, however they need to have an additional rack in between the levels so the water can circulate around all parts of the jars. Once all jars are in the water, cover the water-bath canner with the lid, and increase temperature. Once the water bath begins a rolling boil, set the timer per recipe instructions.

7.

Once processed, turn off the heat and allow the water bath to settle, then carefully remove the hot jars from the water-bath canner, using the jar lifter. I recommend holding a dish towel under the jar to transfer the hot jars from the water bath to the towel-lined counter/table, to avoid any hot water from dripping on you. Do not tilt the jar when removing from the water bath, keep it level. There may be some water caught on the lid of the jar but that is fine, it will evaporate. Allow the jars to cool on a towel-covered surface for 12 hours or more (time varies per recipe). Do not remove clamps or touch the jars until they have completely cooled, otherwise you risk interfering with the jar-sealing process.

8.

Once cooled, the tab on the orange rubber ring should be pointing down; this is one indication that the jar has properly sealed. Remove the clamps and try the "lid-lifting test." Use your fingers to try to gently pull the lid off the base of the jar. The lid should be securely suctioned to the jar and if so, you have successfully sealed the preserve! It is a no-fail way to know for certain your preserve has properly sealed.

9.

To open a sealed jar, remove clamps and use two hands to carefully hold the jar and lid in place while pulling the tab on the orange rubber ring outward. You'll hear the suction break and the lid will remove easily. Once the seal is broken, the jar must be securely closed with the ring, lid, and metal clamps and stored in the refrigerator. Or use a WECK Keep Fresh Cover in place of the rubber ring, lid, and metal clamps.

Before storing your jars, you should label them with the contents and date. If nothing else, just the date so you can keep track of when it was made. Paint pens are convenient and washable. Custom jar labels are unique and cute, especially for gift giving. You can also use a piece of painter's tape and a permanent marker. I always tell myself I'll remember what I made and when I made it, but after years of forgetting, I've learned that labeling is necessary and helpful.

FERMENTATION INGREDIENTS AND SUPPLIES

Before fermenting, run your supplies through the dishwasher or hand wash them with soapy warm water. No need to sanitize tools or vessels when fermenting. Wooden fermenting supplies generally don't require soap. Read instructions that come with the particular product to learn proper care techniques.

Salt: For the purpose of simplicity, every recipe in this book calls for coarse kosher salt. Sea salt is a great option for fermenting, but the amounts vary due to the fine grain of sea salt. Refer to a salt conversion chart when using alternate salt options. Do not use iodized table salt because it is not pure salt.

Water: The purest water you have available to you is the best option. I have a reverse osmosis system at home from which I use water quite often. Water with minerals such as iron could cause discoloration but typically works great. I've fermented with tap water for many years, and it's always been successful with the water from the city where I live. Some chemicals added to city water could possibly cause an adverse reaction to the end product, but you may need to learn by trial and error to know if your tap water will work. If you are in a rural area and have well water as your main source, you can have the water tested to see if there has been any contamination. If you are unsure, store-bought water is also an option.

Common Fermentation Supplies

- Selection of 1-, 2-, 4- and 8-cup measuring cups.
- Measuring spoons in a variety of sizes.
- Stainless-steel wide-mouth funnel for filling jars with fermented foods.
- Clean lint-free towels or paper towels.
- Sharp knife.
- WECK jars in a variety of sizes, typically pint and quart sizes.
- Cutting board.
- Cabbage shredder: optional but helpful.
- Wooden kraut pounder/masher/damper: optional but helpful.
- Food processor to occasionally help streamline a recipe, but not required.
- Weights: lids from smaller WECK jars are excellent weights for fermenting. Even though they aren't super heavy, they usually do a fabulous job of keeping the produce under the brine. Sometimes two lids are needed.

FERMENTING WITH WECK®

Researchers are finding a link between gut bacteria and the rest of the body's overall health, so not only is fermenting your own food a delicious craft, it's also healthy! Fermented foods are generally made at room temperature, and salt is often used to control the spoilage. Fermented foods typically taste tangy and sour. The flavor of a fermented food cannot be compared to anything else; the process of fermentation creates a flavor that cannot be mimicked. Because the fermentation process starts to break down the food, it's easier for the body to digest and the vitamins and nutrients are more readily available for our body to absorb. The live cultures found on lacto-fermented veggies are the same varieties found in our digestive system. Eating a variety of fermented foods offers a variety of good-belly bacteria to our bodies, which is what we need to have a strong, healthy gut biome. To read more about the research being conducted on fermented foods and the link between probiotics and human health, I recommend visiting www.health.harvard.edu.

The Fermentation Process

Brine is the liquid added to a ferment (salt dissolved in water) or the liquid that is naturally created by adding salt to a vegetable (such as sauerkraut). Brine level plays a crucial role in the success of a ferment. The brine always needs to cover the fruit/vegetable that is fermenting by about ¼ to 1 inch. This keeps the ferment from being exposed to air and prevents mold from forming. Low brine level is the main reason ferments go bad, so be adamant about checking the brine level daily.

Headspace is the amount of room between the fermenting food or brine and the rim/lid of the jar. Every fermented recipe requires 1 to 2 inches of headspace because as the produce ferments, carbon dioxide is released, producing small bubbles that can cause the fermenting food to rise in the jar. It's important to check on your ferments every day or two to push the ferment back down and keep the brine level over the produce.

Remove floaters. If you notice small pieces of fruit or vegetable floating up to the surface and hanging out on the top of your brine, use a clean stainless-steel or wooden spoon to scoop out the floater. Floaters make the ferment more susceptible to molding if left in, but if the ferment is a short ferment of 3 days or less, you do not have to worry about them.

Temperature plays a big role in fermentation. As noted in all the fermented recipes in this book, 60 to 75°F (15 to 23°C) is the ideal range for proper fermentation. But keep in mind that the warmer the room is, the quicker fermentation will happen; and conversely, the colder a room is, the slower the fruit or vegetable will ferment. I try to keep my house between 68 and 72°F (20 to 22°C) year-round, as this is the hot-spot range for ferments in my experience. If you do not have air-conditioning in the summer, consider leaving a covered ferment in the basement (if you have one) or a cool corner of your home. Otherwise, plan to do most of your fermenting during the cooler months of the year. You could always ask to keep your ferments at a friend's house; I've done it!

Check on your ferments at least once a day for short-duration fermented recipes and every couple of days for long-duration ferments. Check in on them to make sure the brine remains over the fruit/vegetables. Some recipes throughout the book require "burping" a ferment, which needs to be done daily or multiple times throughout the day. When checking on ferments, you are also looking to make sure no mold or yeast is developing.

Burping the ferment is required in many recipes throughout the book. During the process of fermentation, carbon dioxide is produced and needs to be released to avoid gas buildup and jar breakage. To burp a ferment, simply remove the jar lid, use a clean hand or utensil to stir or push down the fermenting produce, and securely cover the ferment again. It's that simple!

Day 1 of Fermentation

Fermented Pickles: 3 Weeks Later

Cloudy brine and sediment is completely normal and a good thing! When your ferments start the process of fermentation, the brine color will change from clear to cloudy. When fermenting beets, for example, the brine will turn a deep, dark purple. In many ferments you'll see a white sediment on the fermenting produce, or at the bottom of the jar. This is a normal part of the fermentation process, and a sign that things are fermenting as they should.

Kahm yeast is a white thin, powdery-looking film of yeast that occasionally grows on the surface of ferments. It's not harmful but has a strong flavor that most people do not like. If caught early, it's easy to remove by dabbing with a paper towel or scooping out with a spoon. If the yeast is mixed in with the brine, it can cause the taste of the ferment to change. Determine if the kahm yeast has spoiled your ferment by taste testing. The best way to avoid yeast is to check the ferment daily and follow the tips mentioned above.

Tannins are naturally occurring in grape leaves, raspberry leaves, oak leaves, and cherry leaves and that's what helps keep the fermented pickles crunchy. Freeze or dehydrate a few leaves in order to have them on hand year-round. Tannins are also present in horseradish leaves, teas, and bay leaves, however these options will alter the flavor of the overall ferment.

INCLUDE THE CHILDREN!

Create lifelong memories and life skills with the children in your life by including them in the preservation process. Here is a list of tasks that children can do to participate. Little will they know they are learning priceless lessons about food preservation!

Note: Suggested tasks may vary; you are the best judge of your child's capabilities.

Ages 1-3

- Pour measured-out ingredients into jars/pots.
- Rinse off fruits and vegetables.
- Break apart cauliflower florets with hands.
- Taste and smell ingredients and seasonings.

Ages 4-5

- Stir salt into water until dissolved.
- Crank the handle of the apple peeler-corer.
- Using a child-safe serrated knife, children can cut soft fruits and veggies into pieces.
- Use a cherry pitter to pit cherries (very fun!)
- Stir ingredients together.
- Mash fruit with potato masher.
- Peel garlic.
- Mix sauerkraut and salt together.

Age 6+

- Use a real knife to carefully cut vegetables and fruit into uniform-size pieces.
- Grate veggies.
- Scrub produce clean of dirt.
- Measure ingredients.
- Read recipes.
- Stir hot ingredients over stove.
- Peel veggies as needed.
- Pack jars for fermenting.

PART II

WATER-BATH CANNED RECIPES

APPLE PIE JAM

This jam is almost as good as the real deal.

YIELD: 4–5 WECK jam jars (5 cups)

10 cups Granny Smith apples (or other pie-making apple of choice that remains a bit firm after cooking), peeled, cored, and diced
2 cups organic or non-GMO granulated sugar
2 cups brown sugar
2 tsp. ground cinnamon
1 tsp. ground ginger
½ tsp. ground nutmeg

In a large heavy-bottomed pot, mix together all ingredients. Slowly heat the mixture until the sugar is completely dissolved, then increase heat to high and boil for 20 to 25 minutes until the jam and syrup thicken.

Ladle the hot jam into warm prepared jars. Use a funnel to safely transfer the mixture, leaving ½ inch of headspace. Wipe the rims of the jars with a dampened, clean, lint-free cloth or paper towel and again with a dry towel. Place a glass WECK lid with rubber ring in place over the rim of each jar and carefully clip the two metal clamps on each jar directly across from one another.

Add the filled jars to a hot water bath with a rack on the bottom. Place the lid on the canning pot and increase the heat. Once the water bath starts a rolling boil, start the timer and process in the water bath for 10 minutes. Carefully remove the jars from the water bath with a jar lifter and place the jars on a towel-lined surface for 12 hours without touching. After the jars are completely cooled, remove the metal clamps and test the lids to make sure they have securely sealed onto the jars. Label and date jars. Refrigerate after breaking the seal.

NOTES

BLACK-AND-BLUE JAM

Delicious, deep purple jam with tons of flavor.

YIELD: 5 WECK jam jars (5 cups)

4 cups blackberries

4 cups blueberries

4 cups organic or non-GMO granulated sugar

2 tbsp. lemon juice

Wash berries and remove stems and soft/damaged berries. In a large heavy-bottomed nonreactive pot, mix together all ingredients. Bring the mixture to a boil, then reduce to a medium simmer. Simmer about 20 minutes (or double that if using frozen berries) until the jam thickens.

Ladle the hot jam into warm prepared jars. Use a funnel to safely transfer the mixture, leaving ½ inch of headspace. Wipe the rims of the jars with a dampened, clean, lint-free cloth or paper towel and again with a dry towel. Place a glass WECK lid with rubber ring in place over the rim of each WECK jar and carefully clip the two metal clamps on each jar directly across from one another.

Add the filled jars to a hot water bath with a rack on the bottom. Place the lid on the canning pot and increase the heat. Once the water bath starts a rolling boil, start the timer and process in the water bath for 10 minutes. Carefully remove the jars from the water bath with a jar lifter and place the jars on a towel-lined surface for 12 hours without touching. After the jars are completely cooled, remove the metal clamps and test the lids to make sure they have securely sealed onto the jars. Label and date the jars. Refrigerate after breaking the seal.

NOTES

BLUEBERRY CHUTNEY

We enjoy fruit chutney of all kinds, especially served with spicy proteins. This is my take on a blueberry version of this delicious condiment. It's not too sweet and tends to complement whatever dish it is served with. It also pairs well with soft cheeses and a crunchy baguette or crackers.

YIELD: **2–3 WECK jam jars (3 cups)**

4 cups fresh blueberries
½ cup red onion, finely diced
¾ cup brown sugar
¼ tsp. ground ginger
¼ cup golden raisins (optional)
½ cup apple cider vinegar

Wash berries and remove stems and soft/damaged berries. Add the blueberries to a nonreactive pot and, using a potato masher, break down the blueberries. Add all remaining ingredients and mix with the blueberries. Bring the mixture to a boil, then reduce to a medium simmer. Simmer about 15 minutes until the chutney thickens.

Ladle the hot chutney into warm prepared jars. Use a funnel to safely transfer the mixture, leaving ½ inch of headspace. Wipe the rims of the jars with a dampened, clean, lint-free cloth or paper towel and again with a dry towel.

Add the filled jars to a hot water bath with a rack on the bottom. Place a glass WECK lid with rubber ring in place over the rim of each WECK jar and carefully clip the two metal clamps on each jar directly across from one another. Place the lid on the canning pot and increase the heat. Once the water bath starts a rolling boil, start the timer and process in the water bath for 10 minutes. Carefully remove the jars from the water bath with a jar lifter and place the jars on a towel-lined surface for 12 hours without touching. After the jars are completely cooled, remove the metal clamps and test the lids to make sure they have securely sealed onto the jars. Label and date the jars. Refrigerate after breaking the seal.

NOTES

BLUEBERRY AND RHUBARB JAM

Strawberry rhubarb jam has been a favorite of mine for decades, but this combo of blueberries and rhubarb is a close second. Here is another great jam to make when preserving the abundance of rhubarb in the spring. We adoringly nicknamed it "Blubarb Jam."

YIELD: 3–4 jam jars (3½ cups)

2 cups blueberries

4 cups chopped rhubarb

3½ cups organic or non-GMO granulated sugar

2 tbsp. lemon juice

Wash berries and remove stems and soft/damaged berries. Wash and prepare rhubarb. In a large nonreactive pot, mix together all ingredients. Bring the mixture to a boil, then reduce to a medium simmer. Simmer about 15 minutes until the jam thickens.

Ladle the hot jam into warm prepared jars. Use a funnel to safely transfer the mixture, leaving ½ inch of headspace. Wipe the rims of the jars with a dampened, clean, lint-free cloth or paper towel and again with a dry towel.

Add the filled jars to a hot water bath with a rack on the bottom. Place a glass WECK lid with rubber ring in place over the rim of each WECK jar and carefully clip the two metal clamps on each jar directly across from one another. Place the lid on the canning pot and increase the heat. Once the water bath starts a rolling boil, start the timer and process in the water bath for 10 minutes. Carefully remove the jars from the water bath with a jar lifter and place the jars on a towel-lined surface for 12 hours without touching. After the jars are completely cooled, remove the metal clamps and test the lids to make sure they have securely sealed onto the jars. Label and date the jars. Refrigerate after breaking the seal.

NOTES

BROCCOLI PICKLES

These pickles will rank high on your favorite-pickle list, trust me. They are absolutely delicious and a fun and unique way to preserve broccoli. They are delicious in a Bloody Mary, of course, but are also a wonderful addition to salads and relish platters.

YIELD: 2 WECK pint jars (4 cups)

4 cups broccoli florets
6 cloves garlic, halved
2 tsp. dill seed
2 tsp. yellow mustard seeds
2 tsp. red pepper flakes (more for more spice)

BRINE:

1 cup white distilled vinegar (5 percent acidity)
1 cup water
1 tbsp. canning salt

Clean broccoli, remove any damaged or flawed areas, and trim florets to uniform size. In a small nonreactive saucepan, bring the brine ingredients to a boil. Stir until the salt is dissolved and then reduce to a low simmer.

Divide the garlic, dill, mustard seeds, and red pepper flakes between the jars. Pack the jars with broccoli florets and fit them in as snugly as possible without crushing them.

Ladle the brine over the filled jars, leaving ½ inch of headspace. Wipe the rim of the jars with a dampened, clean lint-free cloth or paper towel and again with a dry towel. Place a glass WECK lid with rubber ring in place over the rim of each WECK jar and carefully clip the two metal clamps on each jar directly across from one another.

Add the filled jars to a hot water bath with a rack on the bottom. Place the lid on the canning pot and increase the heat. Once the water bath starts a rolling boil, start the timer and process in the water bath for 10 minutes. Carefully remove the jars from the water bath with a jar lifter and place them on a towel-covered surface for 12 hours without touching. Once completely cooled, remove the metal clamps and test the lids to make sure they have securely sealed onto the jars. Label and date the jars. Allow the broccoli to pickle for at least 2 weeks before opening. The longer they pickle, the more the flavors will meld. Refrigerate after breaking the seal.

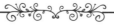

Don't toss the stalk! The stalk of the broccoli is actually my favorite part to eat. Just remove the tough outer layer of the stalk carefully with a paring knife or a potato peeler and enjoy. It is great eaten raw, sautéed, or roasted.

CALI-MIX GIARDINIERA

This colorful blend of vegetables is pickled with serrano peppers to give the veggie medley a mildly spiced flavor. This condiment is great mixed into salads, dips, and chili and is a wonderful addition to sandwiches or stirred into Italian salads.

YIELD: **2 WECK pint jars (4 cups)**

2 cups cauliflower florets
6 serrano peppers, sliced into
¼-inch pieces
4 garlic cloves, finely chopped
1 cup celery, sliced into ¼-inch pieces
2 carrots, cubed or julienned
½ cup red bell pepper, chopped
1 tsp. dried oregano (optional)

BRINE:

2 cups distilled white vinegar (5 percent acidity)
1 cup water
1 tbsp. canning salt

Clean and prepare all vegetables according to ingredient instructions. In a large nonreactive pot, bring the brine ingredients to a boil. Once the salt is dissolved, add the chopped veggies and simmer for 3 minutes, then reduce heat to low.

Use a funnel to carefully ladle the hot vegetable mixture and brine into prepared jars, leaving ½ inch of headspace. Once jars are filled, wipe the rims of the jars with a dampened, clean, lint-free cloth or paper towel and again with a dry towel. Place a glass WECK lid with rubber ring in place over the rim of each WECK jar and carefully clip the two metal clamps on each jar directly across from one another.

Add the filled jars to a hot water bath with a rack on the bottom. Place the lid on the canning pot and increase the heat. Once the water bath starts a rolling boil, start the timer and process in the water bath for 15 minutes. Carefully remove the jars from the water bath with a jar lifter and place the jars on a towel-lined surface for 12 hours without touching. After the jars are completely cooled, remove the metal clamps and test the lids to make sure they have securely sealed onto the jars. Label and date the jars. Refrigerate after breaking the seal.

NOTES

CANDIED JALAPEÑOS

This condiment is sweet and spicy and highly addictive. I like to serve this preserve to guests as an appetizer along with a variety of soft cheeses and crackers. This version of "Cowboy Candy," as some call it, is adapted from a recipe I found in Rebecca Lindamood's cookbook, Not Your Mama's Canning Book.

YIELD: 4–5 WECK jam jars (4 cups)

16 cups (3 lb. whole) jalapeños

SYRUP:

1 ½ cups organic apple cider vinegar

4 cups organic or non-GMO granulated sugar

½ tsp. ground turmeric powder

½ tsp. celery seed

1 tbsp. granulated garlic powder

Wash jalapeños and remove and discard stems. Slice jalapeño peppers into ⅛-inch pieces and collect them in a large bowl. In a large nonreactive pot, mix the syrup ingredients together and bring to a boil. Reduce heat to simmer and stir until the sugar has dissolved. Carefully add all jalapeño slices into the syrup, stir together, and turn heat back up to a boil. Boil for a minimum of 5 minutes. I prefer a tougher texture, so I overcook my jalapeños until they begin to shrivel a bit (this can take 15+ minutes). Determine length of cook time based on your personal preference.

Ladle the hot syrup and pepper slices into warm prepared canning jars, leaving ½ inch of headspace. To avoid a jar full of syrup with few jalapeños, I find it easiest to use a slotted spoon to scoop mostly jalapeño slices into the jars, and to then go back and top off syrup as needed. Use a stainless-steel butter knife or other clean tool to remove any air bubbles trapped within the peppers and the sides of each jar. As the syrup settles between the slices, you may need to add in more.

Wipe the rims of the jars with a dampened, clean, lint-free cloth or paper towel and again with a dry towel. Place a glass WECK lid with rubber ring in place over the rim of each jar and carefully clip the two metal clamps on each jar directly across from one another.

Add the filled jars to a hot water bath with a canning rack on the bottom. Place the lid on the canning pot and increase the heat. Once the water bath starts a rolling boil, start the timer and process in the boiling water bath for 10 minutes (15 minutes if using pint jars instead). Carefully remove the jars from the water bath with a jar lifter and place jars on a towel-lined surface for 12 hours without touching. After 12 hours, when the jars are completely cooled, remove the clamps and test the lids to make sure they have securely sealed onto the jars. Label and date jars. Store in the refrigerator after breaking the seal.

NOTES

CELERY PICKLES

The quart-size cylindrical WECK jar is ideal for this recipe because you can leave the stalks nice and long. These pickled celery stalks make great snacks or garnishes for my favorite drink, a Bloody Mary. See my book WECK Small-Batch Preserving *for the best Bloody Mary mix.*

YIELD: 1 WECK quart jar

1–1 ½ lb. celery (depending on size of celery ribs)
2 cloves garlic, halved
1 tsp. dill seeds
1 tsp. yellow mustard seeds
½ tsp. celery seed
1 tsp. chili flakes (omit if you do not want spice)

BRINE:

1 cup white distilled vinegar (5 percent acidity)
1 cup water
1 tbsp. canning salt

Clean celery, remove any damaged or flawed areas, and trim to fit in a WECK quart jar with about ¾ inch of headspace. Add garlic, dill seeds, mustard seeds, celery seed, and chili flakes (if using) to the bottom of the jar and pack with celery stalks, fitting them in as snugly as possible without crushing them.

In a small nonreactive saucepan, bring the brine ingredients to a boil. Stir until the salt is dissolved and then reduce to a low simmer.

Ladle the brine over the filled jar, leaving ½ inch of headspace. Wipe the rim of the jar with a dampened, clean lint-free cloth or paper towel and again with a dry towel. Place a glass WECK lid with rubber ring in place over the rim of the WECK jar and carefully clip the two metal clamps on the jar directly across from one another.

Add the filled jar to a hot water bath with a rack on the bottom. Place the lid on the canning pot and increase the heat. Once the water bath starts a rolling boil, start the timer and process in the water bath for 10 minutes. Carefully remove the jar from the water bath with a jar lifter and place on a towel-covered surface for 12 hours without touching. Once completely cooled, remove the metal clamps and test that the lid has securely sealed onto the jar. Label and date the jar. Allow the celery to pickle for at least 2 weeks before opening. The longer they pickle, the more the flavors will meld. Refrigerate after breaking the seal.

NOTES

CHUNKY STRAWBERRY AND CHOCOLATE SAUCE

Children and children-at-heart alike enjoy this delicious chocolatey strawberry sauce! We traditionally serve this over vanilla ice cream in our household, but it is also a great topping to spoon over cheesecake, pancakes, waffles, or to bake with.

YIELD: 3 WECK jam jars (3 cups)

4 cups strawberries, quartered

3 cups organic or non-GMO granulated sugar

⅛ cup lemon juice

⅓ cup unsweetened cocoa powder

Wash berries, remove stems, and discard any bruised or flawed berries. Add strawberries to a large heavy-bottomed nonreactive pot and use a potato masher to break down the berries. Mix in sugar and lemon juice and bring to a boil, stirring often. Once the sugar has dissolved, sift in the cocoa powder and mix well. Simmer mixture about 15 minutes until it thickens to a sauce-like consistency.

Ladle the hot strawberry sauce into warm prepared jars. Use a funnel to safely transfer the mixture, leaving ½ inch of headspace. Wipe the rims of the jars with a dampened, clean, lint-free cloth or paper towel and again with a dry towel. Place a glass WECK lid with rubber ring in place over the rim of each WECK jar and carefully clip the two metal clamps on each jar directly across from one another.

Add the filled jars to a hot water bath with a rack on the bottom. Place the lid on the canning pot and increase the heat. Once the water bath starts a rolling boil, start the timer and process in the water bath for 10 minutes. Carefully remove the jars from the water bath with a jar lifter and place them on a towel-covered surface for 12 hours without touching. Once completely cooled, remove the metal clamps and test that the lids have securely sealed onto the jars. Label and date the jars. Refrigerate after breaking the seal.

NOTES

CRANBERRY-APPLE BUTTER

Cranberry apple jam is one of our all-time favorite holiday jams, and this version of fruit butter is a smooth twist on that original recipe (found in WECK Small-Batch Preserving). It doesn't involve peeling the apples, and the end product is absolutely delicious and a gorgeous pinkish red color.

YIELD: 5 WECK jam jars (5 cups)

2½ lb. apples
4 cups cranberries
1 cup apple juice or apple cider
¼ cup pure maple syrup
1 tsp. ground cinnamon
⅛ tsp. ground allspice

Wash apples, remove stems, and cut away any bruised areas. Cut apples into quarters. It's fine to leave seeds and skin intact. Place apples, cranberries, and apple juice or cider in a large heavy-bottomed nonreactive pot and bring ingredients to a simmer. Cook on medium heat with cover on pot and simmer for about 20 minutes until the cranberries are cooked and the apples are soft and can easily be punctured with a fork. Remove from heat and allow to cool slightly.

Use an immersion hand blender or other blender of choice to purée the cran-apple mixture for 1 to 2 minutes until the consistency is smooth and silky. Be careful not to splash any hot mixture on yourself. Use a fine mesh strainer with a glass bowl or large measuring cup beneath to separate the solids from the butter. Once separated, return the cran-apple butter to a large nonreactive pot or saucepan, and add maple syrup, ground cinnamon, and ground allspice. Mix well and heat to simmer. Cook until the consistency is thick and easily spreadable, stir often to avoid burning, and if the consistency is already "apple buttery" after strained, continue to the next step. Using frozen cranberries will add cook time.

Ladle the cran-apple butter into warm prepared jars. Use a funnel to safely transfer the mixture, leaving ½ inch of headspace. Wipe the rims of the jars with a dampened, clean, lint-free cloth or paper towel and again with a dry towel. Place a glass WECK lid with rubber ring in place over the rim of each WECK jar and carefully clip the two metal clamps on each jar directly across from one another.

Add the filled jars to a hot water bath with a rack on the bottom. Place the lid on the canning pot and increase the heat. Once the water bath starts a rolling boil, start the timer and process in the water bath for 10 minutes. Carefully remove the jars from the water bath with a jar lifter and place them on a towel-covered surface for 12 hours without touching. Once completely cooled, remove the metal clamps and test that the lids have securely sealed onto the jars. Label and date jars. Refrigerate after breaking the seal.

DRUNKEN BRANDY OLD-FASHIONED CHERRIES

These cherries are the perfect garnish for the midwestern favorite "Old Fashioned" cocktail. However, they are also perfect on a charcuterie board as a surprisingly scrumptious fruit option.

YIELD: 2 WECK pint jars (4 cups)

2 lb. sweet cherries

⅓ cup organic or non-GMO granulated sugar

⅓ cup water

2 tbsp. lemon juice

½ cup brandy

2 slices orange (optional)

Wash cherries and remove any bruised or flawed areas. Remove stems and pits, leave whole. Mix sugar, water, and lemon juice in a heavy-bottomed nonreactive pot and bring to a medium-high simmer, stirring often until the sugar has dissolved. Once dissolved, add cherries and simmer for 3 minutes. Remove pot from heat and stir in brandy.

Place 1 orange slice in each jar and ladle the hot cherries and syrup into warm prepared jars. Use a funnel to safely transfer the mixture, leaving ½ inch of headspace. Wipe the rims of the jars with a dampened, clean, lint-free cloth or paper towel and again with a dry towel. Place a glass WECK lid with rubber ring in place over the rim of each WECK jar and carefully clip the two metal clamps on each jar directly across from one another.

Add the filled jars to a hot water bath with a rack on the bottom. Place the lid on the canning pot and increase the heat. Once the water bath starts a rolling boil, start the timer and process in the water bath for 10 minutes. Carefully remove the jars from the water bath with the jar lifter and place them on a towel-covered surface for 12 hours without touching. Once completely cooled, remove the metal clamps and test that the lids have securely sealed onto the jars. Label and date the jars. Refrigerate after breaking the seal.

NOTES

ELDERBERRY SYRUP

Elderberries are found in many natural remedies for cold and flu. The berries have immune-boosting properties and are known to cut the duration of colds down by multiple days! Elderberry was almost always the first ingredient in the health concoctions I'd buy, and the tiny one-ounce bottles were very expensive. That's when I decided to start making my own elderberry syrup. It's much more cost-effective to make yourself and can be tailored to your liking. Avoid if you have an allergy or hypersensitivity to elder or honeysuckle plants. I offer two methods of making this syrup. This first method uses pure maple syrup and is water-bath canned for long-term shelf storage. The second method on page 119 is made with raw honey for refrigerator storage.

YIELD: **3 WECK jam jars (3 cups)**

½ cup dried organic elderberries (use 1 cup if using fresh/frozen elderberries)

1 cinnamon stick

1 tsp. ground ginger (or a 1-inch hunk of fresh ginger, peeled)

4 cups water

¾ cup pure maple syrup

2 tbsp. lemon juice

Vanilla extract or bean, or ½ tsp. whole cloves (optional, for different flavor outcomes)

In a medium pot, bring elderberries, cinnamon stick, ginger, and water to a boil, then reduce to a medium-high simmer for 30 minutes. Remove from heat and allow the mixture to cool until lukewarm, then strain through a fine mesh sieve, reserving the liquid in a bowl or measuring cup. Use the back of a spoon to press down on the berries to extract as much liquid as possible. Transfer elderberry liquid into a medium nonreactive saucepan and mix in the maple syrup and lemon juice (and vanilla or cloves) until combined, then reheat syrup, bring to a boil, and remove from heat.

Ladle/pour the hot syrup into warm prepared jars. Use a funnel to safely transfer the mixture, leaving ½ inch of headspace. Wipe the rims of the jars with a dampened, clean, lint-free cloth or paper towel and again with a dry towel. Place a glass WECK lid with rubber ring in place over the rim of each WECK jar and carefully clip the two metal clamps on each jar directly across from one another.

Add the filled jars to a hot water bath with a rack on the bottom. Place the lid on the canning pot and increase the heat. Once the water bath starts a rolling boil, start the timer and process in the water bath for 10 minutes. Carefully remove the jars from the water bath with a jar lifter and place them on a towel-covered surface for 12 hours without touching. Once completely cooled, remove the metal clamps and test that the lids have securely sealed onto the jars. Label and date the jars. Refrigerate after breaking the seal.

The National Center for Home Food Preservation is in the process of updating recommendations for preserving berries (strawberries, blueberries, raspberries, blackberries, etc.) to indicate which fruit species are safe to use with recommended recipes. As elderberries mature this season, check the National Center's website for up-to-date recommendations: https://nchfp.uga.edu/

FALL-SPICED PEACH JAM

The flavor of this jam makes it a perfect fall preserve and one of my bestselling jam blends.

YIELD: 3 WECK jam jars (3 cups)

4 cups peaches, chopped

1 cup organic or non-GMO granulated sugar

2 tbsp. lemon juice

¼ tsp. ground cinnamon

¼ tsp. ground allspice

⅛ tsp. ground cloves (optional)

Wash peaches and remove any bruised or flawed areas. Remove pits and rough chop into 1-inch chunks. Add peaches to a large heavy-bottomed nonreactive pot and use a potato masher to carefully break them down. Add sugar and lemon juice and bring the fruit to a medium simmer. Once simmering, add seasonings. Simmer until the peaches break down and the mixture begins to thicken, about 15 to 20 minutes. Scoop out a small spoonful to cool and taste test to decide if you'd like to add more spices.

Ladle the hot peach jam into warm prepared jars. Use a funnel to safely transfer the mixture, leaving ½ inch of headspace. Wipe the rims of the jars with a dampened, clean, lint-free cloth or paper towel and again with a dry towel. Place a glass WECK lid with rubber ring in place over the rim of each WECK jar and carefully clip the two metal clamps on each jar directly across from one another.

Add the filled jars to a hot water bath with a rack on the bottom. Place the lid on the canning pot and increase the heat. Once the water bath starts a rolling boil, start the timer and process in the water bath for 10 minutes. Carefully remove the jars from the water bath with a jar lifter and place them on a towel-covered surface for 12 hours without touching. Once completely cooled, remove the metal clamps and test that the lids have securely sealed onto the jars. Label and date the jars. Refrigerate after breaking the seal.

NOTES

KETCHUP

I never had any interest in making homemade ketchup. It's sort of time consuming to make and easy to find (and inexpensive) at the grocery store. But once my husband learned he has an intolerance to corn syrup, I decided to make ketchup from fresh tomatoes and can it in the tiny Mini Mold WECK jars so that he could take a serving size of ketchup to go when we dine out. To my surprise, homemade ketchup made with fresh tomatoes is phenomenal and so much better than the store-bought stuff. (I don't know why I was surprised, isn't everything better homemade?) We are totally hooked. However, it takes a lot of tomatoes to yield just a little bit of ketchup, so it's not the most economical use of tomatoes, but it sure is a treat to have in the pantry.

YIELD: **3–4 WECK** jam jars (3–4 cups)

8 lb. fresh tomatoes
1 tsp. garlic powder
1 tsp. onion powder
1 tbsp. canning salt
¼ cup organic or non-GMO granulated sugar
½ cup white distilled vinegar (5 percent acidity)

Wash tomatoes, core (cut around the stem end and remove), cut away any bruised or flawed areas, and quarter. In a large heavy-bottomed nonreactive pot, bring the tomatoes to a boil. You can help move the process along by using a potato masher to mash the tomatoes a bit so they release their juices sooner. Once boiling, cook about 20 minutes until the tomatoes have broken down, then turn off heat and allow to cool slightly. Use an immersion hand blender to purée the mixture. Then, working in batches, use a fine mesh strainer with a nonreactive bowl or large measuring cup (glass, enamel, or stainless steel) underneath to strain the juice from the solids. Use a spoon to stir the mixture around in the strainer to help speed up the process and push the tomato juice through the strainer. Pour the reserved liquid into a large nonreactive saucepan, add in the remaining seasonings, sugar, and vinegar, and bring to a rolling boil. Boil 45 minutes or so, stirring occasionally, until thickened to desired consistency. Once almost done, take a small spoonful out to taste test and determine if you want to add any additional seasonings.

Ladle the ketchup into warm prepared jars. Use a funnel to safely transfer the mixture, leaving ½ inch of headspace. Wipe the rims of the jars with a dampened, clean, lint-free cloth or paper towel and again with a dry towel. Place a glass WECK lid with rubber ring in place over the rim of each WECK jar and carefully clip the two metal clamps on each jar directly across from one another.

Add the filled jars to a hot water bath with a rack on the bottom. Place the lid on the canning pot and increase the heat. Once the water bath starts a rolling boil, start the timer and process in the water bath for 15 minutes. Carefully remove the jars from the water bath with a jar lifter and place them on a towel-lined surface for 12 hours without touching. Once completely cooled, remove the metal clamps and test that the lids have securely sealed onto the jars. Label and date the jars. Refrigerate after breaking the seal. Use within three weeks of breaking the seal.

PEACH AND PLUM JAM

This jam is just as gorgeous as it is delicious. The plum skin offers a nice texture in the spread and adds a colorful tint to the jarred jam. This easy-to-make recipe has become one we make multiple batches of when peaches are available so that we have enough to last the winter.

YIELD: 3 WECK jam jars (3 cups)

3 cups peaches, chopped
1 cup plum, chopped
¾ cup organic or non-GMO granulated
   sugar
2 tbsp. lemon juice

Wash peaches and plums, and remove any bruised or flawed areas. Remove pits and rough chop into 1-inch chunks. Add chopped fruit to a large heavy-bottomed nonreactive pot and use a potato masher to carefully break down the peaches and plums. Add sugar and lemon juice and bring the fruit to a medium simmer. Simmer until the fruit breaks down and the mixture begins to thicken, about 15 to 20 minutes.

Ladle the hot jam into warm prepared jars. Use a funnel to safely transfer the mixture, leaving ½ inch of headspace. Wipe the rims of the jars with a dampened, clean, lint-free cloth or paper towel and again with a dry towel. Place a glass WECK lid with rubber ring in place over the rim of each WECK jar and carefully clip the two metal clamps on each jar directly across from one another.

Add the filled jars to a hot water bath with a rack on the bottom. Place the lid on the canning pot and increase the heat. Once the water bath starts a rolling boil, start the timer and process in the water bath for 10 minutes. Carefully remove the jars from the water bath with a jar lifter and place them on a towel-lined surface for 12 hours without touching. Once completely cooled, remove the metal clamps and test that the lids have securely sealed onto the jars. Label and date the jars. Refrigerate after breaking the seal.

NOTES

PERFECT GARLIC DILL PICKLES:
STEP-BY-STEP

1.

Rinse cucumbers in a 5-gallon food-grade bucket until the water runs clear. Gently swish the cucumbers around with your hand to loosen any dirt or flower buds.

2.

Place the pickling cucumbers in an ice bath for at least 1 hour.

3.

Scrub each cucumber and discard soft or flawed ones.

4.

Trim off the ends of each cucumber. Prep garlic and hot peppers (if using any).

5.

Divide the garlic, dill, and mustard seeds between each jar. Carefully pack with pickles.

6.

Thoughtfully pack jars with cucumbers well, but do not bruise them. Stack them on end to fit.

PERFECT GARLIC DILL PICKLES

This recipe will likely make more brine than you need, but I write it that way for a reason. Not everyone packs jars of pickles equally; some people use a lot of brine and run out mid-recipe. The extra brine can be saved, refrigerated, and reheated to be used again, or it can be used for some quick refrigerator pickles.

YIELD: 5–7 WECK quart jars (amount depends on size of cucumbers)

12 lb. (¼ bushel) small pickling cucumbers freshly harvested within 24–48 hours

2 bulbs garlic, cloves halved

1 jalapeño, quartered or one habanero pepper, halved for a spicy dill pickle (optional)

6 tsp. dill seeds or 1 sprig/head fresh dill per jar

6 tsp. yellow mustard seeds

BRINE:

8 cups distilled white vinegar (5 percent acidity)

8 cups water

¾ cup canning salt

For perfectly crunchy dill pickles, I recommend using small 3-inch pickling cucumbers. Freshness is a crucial part in canning crunchy pickles. Whether you grow them or purchase them from the farmers' market, be sure to only use cucumbers that have been harvested ideally within 24 hours and not more than 48 hours. Feel the cucumbers and make sure they are firm and look fresh; if they are easily bent and manipulated, they are not fresh enough. I repeat: Freshness and size are the key contributors to a crunchy canned pickle.

I keep a 5-gallon food-grade bucket aside for pickle making. Fill the bucket with the cucumbers and use the garden hose to submerge the cucumbers in water. Gently swish the cucumbers around in the water to remove any dirt or flower blooms. Drain out the water (pour it into a garden or yard) and refill the bucket and repeat the process until the water drains out clear. Then, haul the bucket inside the house and fill it with a lot of ice and fresh cold water from the tap. The cucumbers will then take a 1-hour ice bath. While the cucumbers are in the ice bath, prep the garlic and hot peppers (if using).

Once the ice bath is complete, each cucumber will need to be scrubbed by hand. Using a vegetable/fruit bush, scrub away dirt and discard any bruised, soft or damaged cucumbers. Once all are clean, rinse once more with cold water and set aside in a colander until all are cleaned. The next step is to trim off both ends of the cucumber, and any flawed areas.

In a large nonreactive pot, bring the brine ingredients to a boil until the salt is dissolved, then reduce heat to a low simmer. Divide the garlic, dill, and mustard seeds between the prepared jars. I add at least two cloves (4 halves) of garlic to each jar, but feel free to adjust that to your liking by adding more or less. Thoughtfully pack the cucumbers on end, fitting them in as if you were doing a puzzle. Cut larger pickles in half as needed, though I try to avoid this if possible, as the whole pickles tend to stay crunchier. If you are making spicy dill pickles, fit your slices of hot peppers within the cucumbers when packing the jars. Each quart should be well-filled and packed with cucumbers. Depending on what style of WECK jar you are using, you may need to lay a few pickles horizontally to fill the jar, which is fine, just keep the cucumbers below the ½ inch of headspace so that the brine can completely submerge all cucumbers.

Ladle the hot brine into the cucumber-packed jars. Use a funnel to safely transfer the brine into each jar, leaving ½ inch of headspace. Use a stainless-steel butter knife or other nonreactive utensil to rid the jar of any air bubbles trapped between the cucumbers and sides of each jar; add more brine as needed. Wipe the rims of the jars with a clean, dampened, lint-free cloth or paper towel, and again with a dry towel. Place a glass WECK lid and rubber ring on the rim of each WECK jar and carefully clamp the two metal clamps on each jar directly across from one another.

Add the filled jars to a hot water bath with a rack on the bottom. Place the lid on the canning pot and increase the heat. Once the water bath starts a rolling boil, start the timer and process in the water bath for 10 minutes. Carefully remove the jars from the water bath with a jar lifter and place them on a towel-lined surface for 12 hours without touching. Once completely cooled, remove the metal clamps and test that the lids have securely sealed onto each the jars. I recommend letting these pickle for at least 2 months before opening to give the flavors time to meld. Label and date the jars. Refrigerate after breaking the seal.

NOTES

PICKLED BELL PEPPERS

Pickled bell peppers aren't the most common pickle, but you'll be surprised at all the uses you'll find for them. Add them to a sandwich or wrap, chop them up and mix them into salads, or even cook with them. They are delicious added to a homemade pizza. Any variety of bell peppers can be used for this recipe.

YIELD: I WECK pint jar

2 bell peppers
2 cloves garlic, halved

BRINE:

I cup white distilled vinegar (5 percent acidity)
I cup water
½ tsp. canning salt

Wash bell peppers, trim off stems, and remove seeds. Cut away any bruises or blemishes on the peppers. Cut peppers in half and remove white membranes, then slice into ½-inch strips. Trim to fit in the WECK pint jar so that there is ½ inch of headspace.

In a small nonreactive saucepan, bring the brine ingredients to a boil, stir until the salt is dissolved, and reduce heat to a low simmer.

Pack the pepper slices into the jar vertically, fitting as many in as possible without damaging them. Push the garlic slices in between the strips of peppers. Pour the hot brine over the peppers, leaving ½ inch of headspace. Use a stainless-steel butter knife or other nonreactive utensil to rid the jar of any air bubbles trapped between the peppers and the glass jar; add more brine as needed. Wipe the rim of the jar with a clean, dampened, lint-free cloth or paper towel, and again with a dry towel. Place a glass WECK lid and rubber ring on the rim of the WECK jar and carefully clamp the two metal clamps on the jar directly across from one another.

Add the filled jar to a hot water bath with a rack on the bottom. Place the lid on the canning pot and increase the heat. Once the water bath starts a rolling boil, start the timer and process in the water bath for 10 minutes. Carefully remove the jar from the water bath with a jar lifter and place it on a towel-covered surface for 12 hours without touching. Once completely cooled, remove the metal clamps and test that the lid has securely sealed onto the jar. I recommend letting these pickle for at least 2 weeks before opening, as that will give them the flavors time to meld. Label and date the jar. Refrigerate after breaking the seal.

NOTES

PIZZA SAUCE

Level up your homemade pizza game with your own homemade pizza sauce. The best part? You can tailor the flavor to your preference.

YIELD: **3 WECK jam jars (3 cups)**

8 lb. whole tomatoes

2 tsp. garlic powder

1 tsp. onion powder

1 ½ tsp. dried basil

½ tsp. celery seed

1 tbsp. dried oregano

1 tsp. canning salt

1 tbsp. organic or non-GMO granulated sugar

1 tbsp. lemon juice per pint jar (added before canning)

Wash tomatoes, core (cut around the stem end and remove), cut away any bruised or flawed areas, and quarter. In a large heavy-bottomed nonreactive pot, bring the tomatoes to a boil. You can help move the process along by using a potato masher to mash the tomatoes a bit so they release their juices sooner. Once boiling, cook about 20 minutes until the tomatoes have broken down, then turn off heat and allow to cool slightly. Use an immersion hand blender to purée the mixture. Then, working in batches, use a fine mesh strainer with a nonreactive bowl or large measuring cup (glass, enamel, or stainless steel) underneath to strain the juice from the solids. Use a spoon to stir the mixture around in the strainer to help speed up the process and push the tomato juice through the strainer. Pour the liquid into a large nonreactive saucepan, add in seasonings and sugar, and bring to a rolling boil. Boil 35 to 40 minutes until thickened to the desired consistency. Stir occasionally. Once almost done, take a small spoonful out to taste test and determine if you want to add any additional seasonings.

Add 1 tbsp. of lemon juice to each 1-cup or 2-cup WECK jar (add 2 tablespoons of lemon juice per jar if using any jar larger than 2 cups). Ladle the pizza sauce into warm prepared jars. Use a funnel to safely transfer the mixture, leaving ½ inch of headspace. Wipe the rims of the jars with a dampened, clean, lint-free cloth or paper towel and again with a dry towel. Place a glass WECK lid with rubber ring in place over the rim of each WECK jar and carefully clip the two metal clamps on each jar directly across from one another.

Add the filled jars to a hot water bath with a rack on the bottom. Place the lid on the canning pot and increase the heat. Once the water bath starts a rolling boil, start the timer and process in the water bath for 35 minutes (or 40 minutes if using a jar larger than 2 cups). Carefully remove the jars from the water bath with a jar lifter and place them on a towel-covered surface for 12 hours without touching. Once completely cooled, remove the metal clamps and test that the lids have securely sealed onto each jar. Label and date the jars. Refrigerate after breaking the seal. Use within one week of breaking the seal.

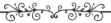

If you decide to preserve in WECK quart-size jars instead of pint jars, adjust the recipe to include 2 tbsp. of lemon juice per quart jar and water-bath process for 40 minutes.

FERMENTED RECIPES

ASPARAGUS PICKLES

Fermented asparagus pickles are a delicious snack straight from the jar, but they are also a suitable substitute for a dill pickle spear as a side with a sandwich or on a relish platter.

YIELD: 1 WECK quart jar (preferably the WECK Cylindrical Jar)

1 ½ lb. asparagus, uniform in thickness if possible
2 sprigs fresh dill
2 garlic cloves, smashed
1 bay leaf
2 thin slices organic lemon (optional)

BRINE:

1 tbsp. kosher salt dissolved in 2 cups of water

Clean the asparagus spears thoroughly and trim off the tough ends to fit into the jar (leave 1 to 2 inches of headspace from the top of the asparagus to the rim of the jar). Add the dill and garlic to the bottom of the jar and pack the jar with the asparagus. It helps to hold the jar sideways so that the asparagus spears can be packed together snugly. Tuck the bay leaf and lemon slices within the asparagus. Be mindful not to crush or bruise the spears.

Pour the brine over the asparagus until it is submerged by at least ¼ inch of brine. Leave 1 to 2 inches of headspace for the weight, brine, and room for the ferment to bubble. Use a lid from a smaller WECK jar (or two lids if needed) and lay them on top of the asparagus spears to completely submerge the asparagus under the brine. Add the WECK jar lid with rubber ring to the WECK jar and secure it shut by adding the two metal clamps directly across from one another. Ferment at room temperature, ideally between 60 to 75°F (15 to 23°C), and keep out of direct sunlight.

This is a 7- to 10-day ferment. Be sure to "burp" the ferment daily to release any built-up carbon dioxide. If the asparagus is above the brine, use a clean finger or utensil to push down on the weight(s) so that all the produce is once again submerged. Once fermentation is complete, transfer to the refrigerator and store in an airtight container with the brine.

NOTES

BREAD-AND-BUTTER PICKLES

This recipe is adapted from my water-bath canned bread-and-butter pickle recipe (found in WECK Small-Batch Preserving), and I'm pretty darn impressed with the outcome. The flavor is very close to the classic vinegar canned, though these b&b pickles have a delicious fermented twist.

YIELD: 1 WECK pint jar

2 cups pickling cucumbers (freshly harvested within 48 hours)
¼ cup yellow onion, very thinly sliced
Ice, as needed
1 tsp. whole yellow mustard seeds
¼ tsp. celery seeds
¼ cup raw honey
¼ tsp. ground turmeric
1 raspberry, oak, or grape leaf (all contain naturally occurring tannins, which will help keep pickles crunchy) (optional)

BRINE:

1 tbsp. kosher salt dissolved into 2 cups water

I recommend using small and firm pickling cucumbers for this recipe (3 to 4 inches in whole form), similar to what you'd use for canned bread-and-butter pickles. Wash pickles, removing any dirt, and trim away any bruised or flawed areas. Discard any soft cucumbers. Slice cucumbers into ¼-inch coins, and prepare onions. Add the sliced cucumbers and onions to a medium sized nonreactive bowl (glass is ideal). Mix together brine ingredients and pour over sliced cucumbers and onions. Add ice as needed for one hour. This ice bath will help keep the cucumber slices crunchy during fermentation. After one hour in the ice bath, strain the cucumber slices and onions, saving and reserving the saltwater for later use.

Add mustard and celery seeds, honey, turmeric, and optional leaf with tannins to the bottom of a clean WECK jar and pack the cucumbers and onions in, leaving 1 inch of headspace. Pour the saltwater over the cucumbers until they are completely submerged, leaving at least ½ inch of headspace. Add a WECK jar lid from a smaller jar to act as a weight to hold down the produce under the brine. Add the glass WECK lid with rubber ring to the rim of the jar, and clip the jar shut with the metal clamps, one directly across from the other. Within 24 hours, the honey at the bottom of the jar will effortlessly dissolve and mix with the rest of the brine. Tip the jar upside down once or twice per day to mix up the ingredients and brine. Store at room temperature, ideally between 60 to 75°F (15 to 23°C), and keep out of direct sunlight.

This is a 4- to 5-day ferment. Be sure to check the ferment once daily to make sure the brine remains over the slices and that no mold or yeast has begun to grow. Taste test to determine when the ferment is done.

Transfer to the refrigerator once you are satisfied with the flavor.

NOTES

CHERRY TOMATOES WITH GARLIC AND FRESH BASIL

This is one of the easiest fermented recipes you'll ever make and one of the most delicious. These tomatoes are enjoyable just hours after mixing them together, but get even more flavor packed after a couple of days (if you can wait that long). They are a delightful addition to pasta, salad, pasta salad, kebab skewers, served with fresh mozzarella, added to a Bloody Mary, or even enjoyed straight from the jar!

YIELD: 1 WECK quart jar

3½ cups cherry tomatoes
5 fresh basil leaves
2 cloves garlic, smashed

BRINE:

1 tbsp. kosher salt dissolved in 2 cups
water

Wash tomatoes and basil with cold water. Put the basil and garlic at the bottom of the jar and fill the jar with cherry tomatoes, leaving 1 to 2 inches of headspace. Pour the brine over the tomatoes, completely submerging them by at least ¼ inch. No weight is needed for this ferment since it is such a short duration. Add the WECK jar lid with rubber ring to the jar and secure the jar shut by adding the two metal clamps directly across from one another. You must "burp" the jar at least once daily to release any built-up carbon dioxide.

Ferment at room temperature, ideally between 60 and 75°F (15 and 23°C), and keep out of direct sunlight. Fermentation duration is between 1 and 3 days. I encourage you to taste a tomato or two just a few hours after mixing things together and then again one day later, again the following day, etc. This will help you determine which taste you prefer and how many days to ferment in the future. Fermentation duration is completely a personal preference of taste. The longer the tomatoes ferment, the softer they will get. Refrigerate with brine in an airtight container once the ideal flavor is reached. It is recommended to eat these tomatoes within a couple of weeks for best texture.

RECIPE VARIATION: CHERRY TOMATOES WITH SLICED ONION AND ROSEMARY

YIELD: 1 WECK quart jar

3½ cups cherry tomatoes
2 sprigs fresh rosemary
2–3 slices yellow onion, thinly sliced

BRINE:

1 tbsp. kosher salt dissolved in 2 cups
water

Follow recipe instructions above, but add onion and rosemary instead of garlic and basil.

GREEN BEANS

This is such a simple recipe, yet very delicious and a great way to preserve the harvest. The beans can be chopped and mixed into salads, added to an appetizer platter, or served on the side like any other pickle. Like most fermented vegetable pickles, they are also a flavorful and healthy snack, straight from the jar.

YIELD: 1 WECK quart jar

½ lb. tender green beans (tough-skinned beans will remain tough)

1 garlic clove, crushed

2 sprigs of fresh dill or 1 tsp. dried (for a garlicky dilly bean ferment) (optional)

BRINE:

1 tbsp. kosher salt dissolved in 2 cups water

Wash the beans and trim off the ends to fit in the jar, leaving 1 to 2 inches of headspace. Place the garlic at the bottom of the jar and pack in the beans vertically. Try to pack the jar as snug as possible without bruising or damaging the beans. During fermentation, the beans will shrink somewhat and begin to float. Once the jar is fully packed, pour the brine over the beans, submerging them completely by at least ¼ inch of brine and leaving at least 1 inch of headspace.

Use a glass lid from a smaller WECK jar (or two, as needed) as a weight to hold the beans underneath the brine. Cover jar with cheesecloth or other breathable cover to keep dust and bugs from entering your ferment or add the glass WECK lid and rubber ring and clamp the jar shut. Be sure to check on the ferment every day to make sure the brine remains over the beans and that no mold has begun to grow. If you are closing the lid on this ferment, be sure to "burp" it 1 or 2 times a day to release the built-up carbon dioxide that is created during fermentation. It is completely normal to see little bubbles or even foam-like bubbling occur at the top of the ferment. If the brine is low, use clean fingers or a utensil to press down the weight(s) to bring the brine back over the ferment.

Ferment at room temperature, ideally between 60 and 75°F (15 and 23°C), and keep out of direct sunlight. This is a 10- to 14-day ferment. Taste test every few days after day 7 to determine when it's "done." If the beans taste raw, like fresh green beans, they are not "done." Once fermentation is complete and the beans are garlicky and tangy to your liking, store in an airtight container or jar with the brine and refrigerate. It is completely normal for the brine to become cloudy and to see sediment appear on the beans or at the bottom of the jar. This is a sign that fermentation is progressing just as it should.

NOTES

CLASSIC FERMENTED DILL PICKLES

Fermented pickles have a very different flavor than vinegar water-bath canned pickles. Many pickle lovers feel very strongly about their preference of one over the other, but most people enjoy both. Fermented pickles are often referred to as "sour" and "half-sour." Those terms reference the amount of time the pickle has fermented. If you are looking for a crunchy half-sour pickle, you will halt fermentation earlier than if you want a fully fermented "sour" pickle. As with canned pickles, I recommend you use freshly harvested cucumbers, ideally cucumbers that have been harvested within 48 hours. This will impact the end result of the firmness of your fermented pickle.

YIELD: 2 WECK quart jars

1–2 lb. 4½–5-inch pickling cucumbers

Ice, as needed

10–15 garlic cloves, crushed

3–4 sprigs or heads fresh dill

2 grape, raspberry, or oak leaves* per quart (the leaves' tannins aid in keeping the pickles crisp) (optional)

2–3 jalapeños, dried chili peppers, or spicier peppers of choice, halved (for spicy garlic dill pickles) (optional)

BRINE:

2 tbsp. kosher salt dissolved in 4 cups water (for a saltier pickle, mix 3 tbsp. kosher salt in 4 cups water)

Gently scrub the pickling cucumbers, removing all flower blossoms and dirt. Discard any soft or blemished cucumbers. Submerge cucumbers in an ice bath for one hour, then strain. Pack the cucumbers, garlic, dill, and optional leaves with tannins into clean WECK jars, leaving 1½ inches of headspace in the jar. Pour the brine over the cucumbers, and add a lid (or two, as needed) a from a smaller WECK jar as a weight to keep the produce submerged under the brine, leaving at least 1 inch of headspace.

Place the glass WECK lid with rubber ring in place over the rim of each WECK jar and carefully clip the two metal clamps on each jar directly across from one another. Ferment at room temperature, ideally between 60 and 75°F (15 and 23°C), and keep out of direct sunlight. Be sure to check on the ferment daily to make sure the brine remains over the cucumbers and that no mold or yeast has begun to grow. Be sure to "burp" the ferment 1 or 2 times a day to release the built-up carbon dioxide. It is completely normal to see little bubbles or even foam-like bubbling occur at the top of the ferment. If the produce has floated above the brine level, use a clean finger or utensil to press down the weight(s) to bring the brine back over the ferment.

This is a 7- to 30-day ferment. The time frame ranges greatly because there are a few things to take into consideration: 1. Temperature: If you are fermenting in the middle of summer and the kitchen is warm, the pickles will ferment faster, 2. Freshness and size of the cucumber, and 3. Taste: If you are hoping for a crunchy half-sour, you will ferment for less time than a full sour pickle, which will take closer to 3 to 4 weeks to fully ferment. As the pickles ferment, the brine will become cloudy and you may notice sediment on the pickles or at the bottom of the jar—this is all completely normal and it is a sign that fermentation is happening just as it should. As the cucumbers ferment into pickles, they will turn from a bright green to a dull green—this is also a sign that fermentation is progressing properly.

If you think that your fermented pickles may be done, the best way to tell is to taste test one. If it has a raw cucumber flavor, close the jar, allow the cucumbers to continue to ferment, and taste test again in a few days. Once fermentation is complete, transfer the jar to the refrigerator with the brine.

*You can certainly make fermented pickles without the added leaves, but the naturally occurring tannins found in grape, raspberry, and oak leaves help keep cucumbers crisp during fermentation. Horseradish leaves, bay leaves, and black tea also offer tannins (1 tea bag per quart), but these options will alter the flavor of the pickle ferment. Keep in mind that too many leaves with tannins will result in a mushy pickle, so be sure to just add a couple leaves per quart jar.

Day 1   *Day 21*

HOT PEPPER SAUCE: STEP-BY-STEP

1.

Once peppers are fermented and ready for step 2, drain the peppers and garlic from the brine, reserve the brine, and set aside. Purée with ¼ cup brine until completely broken down.

2.

Strain out the solids, reserving the hot sauce.

3.

Transfer hot pepper liquid into a clean, airtight WECK jar and refrigerate. Enjoy!

HOT PEPPER SAUCE

This particular recipe uses jalapeño peppers, but the basic guidelines of how to make it can be applied to any hot pepper(s) of your choice. A variety of mixed peppers gives this hot sauce layers of flavor. Have fun and experiment!

YIELD: 1 WECK pint jar of finished hot sauce

4 cups jalapeño or other hot peppers
1 WECK quart jar (needed during fermentation)
10 garlic cloves, crushed

BRINE:

1½ tbsp. kosher salt dissolved in 3 cups water

Wash the jalapeños and remove the stems and any flawed areas from the peppers. Slice the peppers in half lengthwise. Pack a WECK quart jar tightly with the hot peppers and garlic.

Pour the brine over the jalapeños until they are completely submerged, leaving 1 to 2 inches of headspace. Use one or two lids from a smaller WECK jar to completely weigh down the peppers under the brine. Place the glass WECK lid with rubber ring in place over the rim of the jar and carefully clip the two metal clamps on the jar directly across from one another. Ferment at room temperature, ideally between 60 and 75°F (15 and 23°C), and keep out of direct sunlight. Check on the ferment every day to make sure the brine remains over the peppers and that no mold or yeast has begun to grow. Be sure to "burp" it 1 or 2 times a day to release the built-up carbon dioxide. It is completely normal to see little bubbles or even foam-like bubbling occur at the top of the ferment. If the peppers have floated up over the brine level, use a clean utensil to press down the weight(s) to bring the brine back over the ferment.

This is a 3-week (or longer) ferment. At the 3-week mark, I recommend you smell the ferment and even taste the brine. Does it have good flavor? Is it spicy? Have the jalapeños turned from a bright green (as they looked on day one) to a dulled green, almost brownish-green color? If you are answering no to these questions, you may want to consider allowing the peppers to ferment another week, and ask yourself these questions again. If the ferment smells great and the brine is spicy and flavorful, move on to the final steps of this process.

Once you are ready to turn the fermented peppers into hot sauce, you must drain the brine from the hot peppers and garlic, reserving the brine. Pour the brine into a measuring cup and set it aside. Using a food processor, blend the jalapeños and garlic with ¼ cup of brine and purée it. If the peppers are not breaking down easily in the food processor, add additional brine until things are blending smoothly.

Once all of the peppers and garlic are puréed, use a fine mesh strainer to strain out the solids. Place the sieve over a large measuring cup. Pour the pepper purée into the sieve and separate the solids. Use the back of a spoon to push the purée into the strainer; get as much liquid out of the mash as you can.

The drained liquid is your hot sauce. Once all the liquid is collected, transfer the hot sauce into a clean, airtight WECK jar with the lid securely clamped on and refrigerate.

RECIPE VARIATION: ADDITIONAL INGREDIENTS

For an extremely fiery hot sauce, use a mix of habanero, Thai, serrano, or other hot peppers available to you. Feel free to experiment with adding some onions, fruits, herbs, or other vegetables to create new hot sauce flavors. Just remember to take note of your experimental recipes so you can re-create the best ones!

BONUS RECIPE: DEHYDRATED PEPPER SOLIDS

Don't toss those pepper solids—dehydrate them! Once dehydrated, you can use them as-is or blend into a powder with a coffee/seasoning grinder. To dehydrate in a food dehydrator, first make sure you are in a well-ventilated area. Spread the pulp onto a dehydrator sheet in a ⅛- to ¼-inch-thick layer and set the temperature to 125°F (52°C) for 8+ hours until the solids have become completely dried out. Store in an airtight jar.

NOTES

PEACH SALSA

This salsa is the perfect summertime salsa. It's great at a BBQ served with corn chips or sprinkled over fish tacos for a pop of flavor.

YIELD: 1 WECK quart jar (3 cups finished salsa)

3 cups yellow peaches (not overly ripe), pits removed, diced
1 cup onion, diced
¼ cup jalapeños, diced
1 clove garlic, finely chopped
½ tsp. kosher salt
1 lime, juiced
½ cup cilantro, chopped

Prepare all ingredients and mix them together in a large nonreactive bowl. Pack the mixture into a WECK quart-size jar. Use a lid (or two) from a smaller WECK jar as a weight to hold the salsa underneath the brine. Place the glass WECK lid with rubber ring in place over the rim of the jar and carefully clip the two metal clamps on the jar directly across from one another.

Ferment at room temperature, ideally between 60 and 75°F (15 and 23°C), and keep out of direct sunlight. Fermentation duration is between 12 and 48 hours, though the salsa is delicious immediately after mixing together. I encourage you to taste the ferment initially after mixing it together, then again the next day and again the following day so you can experience the flavor transform. This will help you determine which taste you prefer and how many days to ferment in the future (make a note below)! Fermentation duration is completely a personal preference of taste. Once the ideal flavor is reached, store the jar in the refrigerator. Eat within 2 weeks, as fruit-based ferments do not last long.

NOTES

RADISH SALSA

This salsa is delicious immediately after the ingredients are mixed together but gets prettier and more flavorful after fermentation. Many people who are not fond of radishes in the raw form enjoy fermented radishes, as the raw radish flavor dulls somewhat. I urge you to try this salsa even if radishes aren't on the top of your list. Use this salsa as you would any other salsa; over eggs, with corn chips, or over tacos.

YIELD: 1 WECK pint jar

1 bundle (1½ cups) red radishes, chopped
2 (¼ cup) scallions, thinly sliced
¼ cup fresh cilantro, chopped
½ jalapeño, finely diced
1 tsp. kosher salt
Dash black pepper (optional)

Prepare all ingredients and mix them together in a large glass or nonreactive bowl. Pack the mixture into a WECK pint-size jar. Use a lid (or two) from a smaller WECK jar as a weight to hold the salsa underneath the brine. It may take until the next day for the ferment to produce enough brine to submerge the radishes, so don't be alarmed if they aren't initially submerged. Place the glass WECK lid with rubber ring in place over the rim of the jar and carefully clip the two metal clamps on the jar directly across from one another.

Ferment at room temperature, ideally between 60 and 75°F (15 and 23°C), and keep out of direct sunlight. Fermentation duration is between 5 and 7 days, though the salsa is delicious immediately after mixing together. One sign that the ferment is "done" is when the brine becomes pink. Taste test after day 5. Once the ideal flavor is reached, store the jar in the refrigerator with the brine.

NOTES

SAUERKRAUT: STEP-BY-STEP

1.

Remove outer cabbage leaves, clean, slice in half, remove core, and shred cabbage into thin shreds.

2.

Add salt and gently massage salt into shreds. Once you can squeeze brine from the shreds, you are ready to pack your jar.

3.

Tightly pack the shredded cabbage into a WECK jar, leaving 1 to 2 inches of head-space. Pour any remaining brine into the jar as well.

4.

Use a lid from a smaller WECK jar as a weight to hold the cabbage shreds under the brine. Then, add the rubber ring and glass WECK lid and clip on the metal clamps.

SAUERKRAUT

Here is the method for making classic "naked" sauerkraut. Feel free to experiment with different seasonings or by adding in different vegetables to create new sauerkraut flavors.

YIELD: 1 WECK quart

1 head (2–2½ lb.) organic green
    cabbage
1–2 tbsp. kosher salt

Remove the outer leaves from the cabbage and discard. Wash the cabbage with cold water. Cut the cabbage in half lengthwise and remove the core from each half. Shred the cabbage into thin shreds ⅛-inch thick or thinner. Reserve shredded cabbage in a large nonreactive pot or bowl.

Once completely shredded, mix in the salt. Use clean hands (remove jewelry and nail polish before this step, or wear powder-free food-prep gloves) to massage the salt into the shreds. Squeeze and mix for several minutes until you are able to squeeze a handful of cabbage and liquid drips out—this is the natural brine that is created through the "dry salting" method. It could take several minutes of mixing and massage before the brine is created, it just depends on how fresh the cabbage is.

Transfer the cabbage into a clean WECK quart jar and push down with your fist as you pack the jar. It's helpful to use a regular-mouth funnel when packing the jar, as it creates less mess. Pack the jar tightly and pour any brine remaining in the bowl over the cabbage shreds, leaving 1 to 2 inches of headspace in the jar. If there is not enough brine to cover the cabbage initially, likely by the next day there will be plenty. Use a small WECK lid or two from a smaller WECK jar to act as weight(s) to hold the cabbage under the brine. Clean the rim of the jar and apply the glass WECK lid with rubber ring and clip the clamps on the jar directly across from one another.

Be sure to check on the kraut daily to make sure the brine remains over the shreds of cabbage and that no mold has begun to grow. You will need to open the lid 1 or 2 times per day to "burp" the ferment and allow the built-up gas to release. It is completely normal to see little bubbles or foam-like bubbling occur at the top of the ferment. During fermentation, little gas bubbles get trapped between the cabbage shreds, which pushes the cabbage upward in the jar. If the cabbage rises above the brine level, use a clean finger or utensil to push the weight(s) down so that brine once again covers the cabbage.

Ferment at room temperature, ideally between 60 and 75°F (15 and 23°C), and keep out of direct sunlight. This is a 2- to 4-week ferment. Weekly taste testing is recommended to determine when the kraut is "done," and which flavor you prefer. The kraut should taste sour and tangy, not like raw cabbage. The fermentation time frame varies largely on the temperature; cool temperatures will take longer to ferment, warm temperatures will ferment faster. Additional ingredients will also play a part in fermentation duration, and ultimately the point at which the sauerkraut is "done" is determined by personal preference. Once the sauerkraut is done to your liking, store in an airtight container (or in the jar) with the brine and refrigerate.

NOTES

HAWAIIAN KRAUT

When I was taking my Master Preserver Certification Course in Kona-Kailua, Hawaii, occasionally after class we'd grab a quick bite to eat from a local burrito restaurant. Everything was made from scratch and made to order. This recipe is inspired by the "pineapple slaw" that I'd get on my burritos. It is traditionally made with mayonnaise, as is the ever-popular coleslaw on the mainland, though this is my fermented twist on the adored Hawaiian slaw.

YIELD: 1 WECK quart jar
(3–4 cups)

1 head (2–2½ lb.) organic
  green cabbage

1–2 (½ cup) carrots, grated

½ cup fresh pineapple,
  grated

½ cup yellow onion, thinly
  sliced

¼ cup fresh cilantro,
  chopped

¼ tsp. ground black pepper

1 tbsp. kosher salt

Remove the outer leaves from the cabbage and discard. Wash the cabbage with cold water. Cut the cabbage in half lengthwise and remove the core from each half. Shred the cabbage into thin shreds ⅛-inch thick or thinner. Reserve shredded cabbage in a large nonreactive pot or bowl.

Sprinkle the salt over the cabbage and mix together (remove jewelry and nail polish before this step, or wear powder-free food-prep gloves). Massage the salt into the cabbage shreds until you are able to squeeze a handful of cabbage and liquid drips away; this is the natural brine that is created through the process of "dry salting." This process could take a few minutes or take many, it just depends on how fresh the cabbage is. Be careful not to turn your cabbage into mush, because the end product will be a mushy sauerkraut.

Once the natural brine is created, add in the remaining ingredients and mix together well. Transfer the cabbage mixture into a clean WECK quart jar and push down with your fist as you pack the jar. It's helpful to use a regular-mouth funnel when packing the jar, as it creates less mess. Pack the jar tightly and pour any brine remaining in the bowl over the cabbage shreds, leaving 1 to 2 inches of headspace in the jar. If there is not enough brine to cover the cabbage initially, likely by the next day there will be plenty. Use a small WECK lid or two from a smaller WECK jar to act as weight(s) to hold the cabbage under the brine. Clean the rim of the jar and apply the glass WECK lid with rubber ring and clip the clamps on the jar directly across from one another.

Be sure to check on the kraut daily to make sure the brine remains over the shreds of cabbage and that no mold has begun to grow. You will need to open the lid 1 or 2 times per day to "burp" the ferment and allow the built-up gas to release. It is completely normal to see little bubbles or foam-like bubbling occur at the top of the ferment. During fermentation, little gas bubbles get trapped between the cabbage shreds, which pushes the cabbage upward in the jar. If the cabbage rises above the brine level, use a clean finger or utensil to push the weight(s) down so that brine once again covers the cabbage.

Ferment at room temperature, ideally between 60 and 75°F (15 and 23°C), and keep out of direct sunlight. This is a 10- to 14-day ferment. Taste test every few days after day 7 to determine when it's "done." If it tastes like raw produce, it is not "done." Once fermentation is complete, store in an airtight container or jar and refrigerate.

LATE-SUMMER KRAUT

This kraut combines the flavors you'll find in Minnesota at the end of summer—fresh corn and fennel. You can even finely slice up some leeks for a different flavor.

YIELD: 1 WECK quart

½ head green or purple cabbage, finely shredded

½ bulb fennel, fronds removed, finely chopped

1 cup fresh corn kernels

1 tbsp. kosher salt

Remove the outer leaves from the cabbage and discard. Wash the cabbage with cold water. Cut the cabbage in half lengthwise and remove the core from each half. Shred the cabbage into thin shreds ⅛-inch thick or thinner. Reserve shredded cabbage in a large nonreactive pot or bowl.

Sprinkle the salt over the cabbage and mix together (remove jewelry and nail polish before this step, or wear powder-free food-prep gloves). Massage the salt into the cabbage shreds until you are able to squeeze a handful of cabbage and liquid drips away, this is the natural brine that is created through the process of "dry salting." This process could take a few minutes or take many, it just depends on how fresh the cabbage is. Be careful not to turn your cabbage into mush, because the end product will be a mushy sauerkraut.

Once the natural brine is created, add in the remaining ingredients and mix together well. Transfer the cabbage mixture into a clean WECK quart jar and push down with your fist as you pack the jar. It's helpful to use a regular-mouth funnel when packing the jar, as it creates less mess. Pack the jar tightly and pour any brine remaining in the bowl over the cabbage shreds, leaving 1 or 2 inches of headspace in the jar. If there is not enough brine to cover the cabbage initially, likely by the next day there will be plenty. Use a small WECK lid or two from a smaller WECK jar to act as weight(s) to hold the cabbage under the brine. Clean the rim of the jar and apply the glass WECK lid with rubber ring and clip the clamps on the jar directly across from one another.

Be sure to check on the kraut daily to make sure the brine remains over the shreds of cabbage and that no mold has begun to grow. You will need to open the lid 1 or 2 times per day to "burp" the ferment and allow the built-up gas to release. It is completely normal to see little bubbles or foam-like bubbling occur at the top of the ferment. During fermentation, little gas bubbles get trapped between the cabbage shreds, which pushes the cabbage upward in the jar. If the cabbage rises above the brine level, use a clean finger or utensil to push the weight(s) down so that brine once again covers the cabbage.

Ferment at room temperature, ideally between 60 and 75°F (15 and 23°C), and keep out of direct sunlight. This is a 2- to 3-week ferment. Taste test every few days after day 7 to determine when it's "done." If it tastes like raw produce, it is not "done." Once fermentation is complete, clamp on the jar lid and refrigerate.

DILL AND GARLIC KRAUT

Garlic-dill pickles are my favorite, so I knew this kraut would be a hit. Garlic and dill are a match made in heaven. This kraut is a good snack but also goes especially well with anything you'd normally serve a pickle with.

3 garlic cloves (1 tbsp.), chopped
1 tbsp. dill weed, chopped

Follow the directions for Sauerkraut (pg. 90), but add in garlic and dill before jarring and fermenting. This recipe takes 2 to 3 weeks to ferment.

DILL AND LEMON KRAUT

This refreshing sauerkraut is fantastic paired with fish and other seafood.

1 tbsp. dill weed, chopped
Juice of 1 lemon (reserve a few thin slices to add to jar)

Follow the directions for Sauerkraut (pg. 90), but add in lemon and dill before jarring and fermenting. This recipe takes 2 to 3 weeks to ferment.

NOTES

ITALIAN SAUERKRAUT

This recipe was created by Wendy and Sue of NW Ferments. They are Oregon-based friends with a passion for fermented foods. They grow and sell their starter cultures as well as fermentation supplies through their website www.nwferments.com and at natural food stores throughout the country. Wendy and Sue say "This sauerkraut brings together wonderful flavors of Italy. It's great mixed in pastas, salads, soups, deli sandwiches, or eaten as a side dish with Italian sausage. We think it's 'Saporito!'"

YIELD: 1 WECK quart

1 head (2–2½ lb.) green
   cabbage
½ cup fennel, thinly sliced,
   fronds optional
½ cup onion, thinly sliced
3 (1 tbsp.) garlic cloves, minced
½ tsp. dried basil
½ tsp. dried oregano
1 cup tomato, peeled, deseeded,
   thinly sliced (optional)
¼ tsp. dried chili flakes
   (optional)

Remove the outer leaves from the cabbage and discard. Wash the cabbage with cold water. Cut the cabbage in half lengthwise and remove the core from each half. Shred the cabbage into thin shreds ⅛-inch thick or thinner. Reserve shredded cabbage in a large nonreactive pot or bowl. Add in fennel and mix.

Sprinkle the salt over the cabbage and fennel, and mix together (remove jewelry and nail polish before this step, or wear powder-free food-prep gloves). Massage the salt into the cabbage shreds until you are able to squeeze a handful of cabbage and liquid drips away, this is the natural brine that is created through the process of "dry salting." This process could take a few minutes or take many, it just depends on how fresh the cabbage is. Be careful not to turn your cabbage into mush, because the end product will be a mushy sauerkraut.

Once the natural brine is created, add in the remaining ingredients and mix together well. Transfer the cabbage mixture into a clean WECK quart jar and push down with your fist as you pack the jar. It's helpful to use a regular-mouth funnel when packing the jar, as it creates less mess. Pack the jar tightly and pour any brine remaining in the bowl over the cabbage shreds, leaving 1 to 2 inches of headspace in the jar. If there is not enough brine to cover the cabbage initially, likely by the next day there will be plenty. Use a small WECK lid or two from a smaller WECK jar to act as weight(s) to hold the cabbage under the brine. Clean the rim of the jar and apply the glass WECK lid with rubber ring and clip the clamps on the jar directly across from one another.

Be sure to check on the kraut daily to make sure the brine remains over the shreds of cabbage and that no mold has begun to grow. You will need to open the lid 1 or 2 times per day to "burp" the ferment and allow the built-up gas to release. It is completely normal to see little bubbles or foam-like bubbling occur at the top of the ferment. During fermentation, little gas bubbles get trapped between the cabbage shreds, which pushes the cabbage upward in the jar. If the cabbage rises above the brine level, use a clean finger or utensil to push the weight(s) down so that brine once again covers the cabbage.

Ferment at room temperature, ideally between 60 and 75°F (15 and 23°C), and keep out of direct sunlight. This is a 10- to 14-day ferment. Taste test every few days after day 7 to determine when it's "done." If it tastes like raw produce, it is not "done." Once fermentation is complete, securely clamp the lid on the jar and refrigerate.

STRAWBERRY-BASIL SALSA

Delicious and pretty, this summery salsa is a welcomed condiment over fish, eaten with chips, or enjoyed with a soft cheese and crackers.

YIELD: 1 WECK pint jar

2 cups fresh strawberries, stems
 removed, diced
2 tbsp. red onion, finely chopped
1 tsp. fresh lemon juice
¼ cup fresh basil, finely chopped
1 jalapeño, finely chopped (optional)
⅛ tsp. kosher salt

Prepare all ingredients and mix them together in a large nonreactive bowl. Pack the mixture into a WECK pint jar, leaving 1 to 2 inches of headspace. Place the glass WECK lid with rubber ring in place over the rim of the jar and carefully clip the two metal clamps on the jar directly across from one another.

Ferment at room temperature, ideally between 60 and 75°F (15 and 23°C), and keep out of direct sunlight. Fermentation duration is between 2 and 3 days. I encourage you to taste the ferment at day 2, and again the following day, etc. This will help you determine which taste you prefer and how many days to ferment in the future. Fermentation duration is completely a personal preference of taste. Once the flavor is ideal, store the jar in the refrigerator. Eat within 2 weeks.

NOTES

SWEET CORN RELISH

This crunchy sweet corn relish is delicious on everything! Through fermentation, the corn stays sweet and crisp, but the flavors meld together and create a delicious bubbly, fermented version of classic corn relish. It is by far one of my all-time favorite ferments.

YIELD: 1 WECK quart jar

3–4 whole ears (2½ cups) fresh corn kernels

½ cup bell pepper, diced

¼ cup yellow onion, finely chopped

BRINE:

1 tbsp kosher salt dissolved in 2 cups water

Shuck and rinse corn. Shave the kernels off the cob. Prep bell pepper and onion, mix together with corn, and transfer to a quart WECK jar, leaving 1 to 2 inches of headspace. Mix brine and pour over corn mixture until completely submerged. Place the glass WECK lid with rubber ring on the rim of the WECK jar and clip the jar shut with the two clamps directly across from one another.

Ferment at room temperature, ideally between 60 and 75°F (15 and 23°C), and keep out of direct sunlight. Be sure to "burp" this ferment 1 or 2 times a day to release the built-up carbon dioxide. It is completely normal to see little bubbles or even foam-like bubbling occur at the top of the ferment. Fermentation duration is between 2 and 4 days. I encourage you to taste the ferment at day 2, and again the following day, etc. This will help you determine which taste you prefer and how many days to ferment in the future. Fermentation duration is completely a personal preference of taste. Once the flavor is ideal, store the jar in the refrigerator with the brine.

NOTES

ZUCCHINI PICKLES

If you grow zucchini in your garden, you more than likely get to a point where you wonder how to use it all up. Or perhaps you lose track of one and find it when it's the size of a baseball bat? Either way, this recipe is a perfect one for your extra zucchini. This recipe was born when my uncle offhandedly told me that he preferred fermented zucchini pickles to cucumber dills. I immediately went home and prepped a batch and, I'll be darned, it's definitely a good pickle. I'll never agree that it's better than cucumber pickles (because they are my favorite) but I'm positively a fan of this alternative dill pickle. I prefer to use the larger, more tough-skinned zucchinis for this recipe.

YIELD: 1 WECK quart jar

1 lb. zucchini
2–4 garlic cloves, smashed
2 sprigs fresh dill

BRINE:

1 tbsp. kosher salt dissolved in 2 cups water

Wash zucchini, trim ends, and remove any flawed areas. No need to peel the skin. Halve/quarter the zucchini lengthwise. Cut to size so that the zucchini spears fit into the jar lengthwise, with 1 to 2 inches of headspace between the zucchini and rim of jar.

Place garlic and dill in the bottom of the jar, and pack it with the zucchini spears, fitting them in vertically as snug as possible without bruising or smashing the spears. Once the jar is packed, pour the brine over the spears until they are covered by at least ¼ inch of brine. Use a lid from a smaller WECK jar as a weight to hold the produce under the brine. Place the WECK lid with rubber ring on the rim of the WECK jar and clip the jar shut with clamps directly across from one another.

Ferment at room temperature, ideally between 60 and 75°F (15 and 23°C), and keep out of direct sunlight. Be sure to "burp" the ferment 1 or 2 times a day to release the built-up carbon dioxide. It is completely normal to see little bubbles or even foam-like bubbling occur at the top of the ferment. Fermentation duration is 7 to 10 days. I encourage you to taste the ferment at day 7 to see if the spears have transformed into a delicious, garlicky dill pickle. If they still taste like raw zucchini, allow them to ferment another day or two and taste test again. Once the flavor is ideal, store the jar in the refrigerator with the brine.

If using an overgrown zucchini with large, firm seeds, just use a spoon to scrape the seeds out and ferment as directed in the recipe.

MADE-FROM-SCRATCH RECIPES

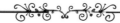

Note: The following recipes are not water-bath canned or fermented.

BLUE CHEESE DRESSING

Upgrade your next salad with this homemade blue cheese dressing.

YIELD: 1 WECK pint jar

¼ cup mayonnaise or vegan mayo
¼ cup plain whole milk Greek yogurt
1 tbsp. white wine vinegar
3 tbsp. buttermilk
1 cup blue cheese crumbles, divided
Pinch of ground black pepper

Add all ingredients to a blender (reserving ½ cup of blue cheese crumbles to mix in at the end) and blend for 30 seconds, or until all ingredients are thoroughly mixed together. Transfer to a clean WECK jar and stir in the reserved blue cheese crumbles. Add the glass WECK lid with rubber ring onto the rim of the jar and clip the jar shut with clamps directly across from one another. Refrigerate and use within 2 weeks.

NOTES

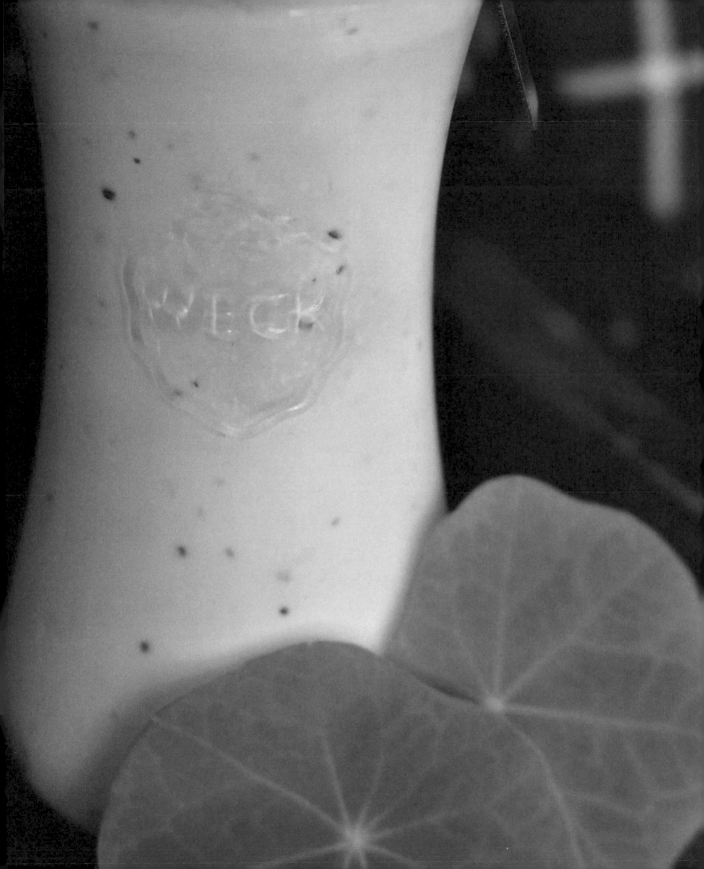

PEPPERCORN RANCH DRESSING

This ranch will knock your socks off. You'll never want the store-bought stuff again. I note "vegan mayo" as an option in the recipe because my husband cannot eat chicken eggs, and the vegan mayo is a seamless substitute.

YIELD: 1 WECK pint jar

¼ cup mayonnaise or vegan mayo
¼ cup plain whole milk Greek yogurt
¼ cup cottage cheese
3 tbsp. buttermilk
1 garlic clove
1 ½ tsp. white wine vinegar
¼ tsp. kosher salt
½ tsp. ground black pepper

Add all ingredients to a blender and blend for 30 seconds, or until all ingredients are thoroughly mixed together. Transfer to a clean WECK jar, add the glass WECK lid with rubber ring onto the rim of the jar, and clip it securely closed with the two metal clamps, one directly across from the other. Refrigerate and use within 2 weeks.

NOTES

COFFEE LIQUEUR

This homemade coffee liqueur is better than any store-bought version and much more cost-effective. We use the liqueur to make our favorite holiday cocktails and bottle up a couple extra batches to give as gifts. Why drink corn syrup and caramel color when you can make it homemade with just a few ingredients?

YIELD: 2 WECK pint jars (about 4½ cups) or WECK juice jars

4 cups water

2½ cups organic or non-GMO granulated sugar

4 tbsp. instant coffee

1 tbsp. vanilla extract or 1 vanilla bean, sliced down the center

2½ cups white rum

Mix water, sugar, and coffee together in a pot. Use a larger pot than you'd need for that amount of liquid, because I learned the hard way that this recipe can quickly boil over if you're not careful. Simmer the mixture uncovered for 30 to 60 minutes. I give a wide range of time here because if you are simmering on high, it cooks faster and you risk boiling over. Simmering at a lower temperature will take longer, but you give yourself more leeway to catch a boil-over. Stir often.

Once the mixture looks like it's thickening and more syrup-like, dip a spoon in the syrup and set it aside to cool. Once cooled, test the syrup by dragging your finger through it; if you can make a line through it without the syrup falling back into place, it has thickened enough. Remove syrup from heat and allow to cool. Once cooled, pour the coffee syrup into a large measuring cup. Stir in vanilla extract (if using a vanilla bean, add when jarring liqueur). Whatever amount it measures, add exactly the same amount of rum. For example, if you made 3 cups of coffee syrup, add 3 cups of rum. Stir until completely mixed.

Transfer to an airtight WECK jar or two (I prefer the juice jars) and store in a dark, room-temp place as you'd keep any other liquor.

For other coffee liqueur flavor outcomes, consider mixing the coffee syrup with equal parts of vodka, brandy, or whiskey instead of rum.

BONUS RECIPE: WHITE RUSSIAN

This is our favorite holiday cocktail using this coffee liqueur.

2 ounces coffee liqueur

2 ounce vodka

2 ounces half-and-half or whole milk

Fill a lowball glass with ice, add coffee liqueur and vodka, mix, then top with half-and-half or whole milk (or for less calories, use skim or soy milk), and serve.

Infused 1 month

Infused 3 months

VANILLA EXTRACT

Homemade vanilla extract is unbelievably easy to make; the hardest part is waiting for the flavor to infuse. With vanilla extract priced so high, it is much more affordable to make your own. Have you ever wondered why vanilla beans are so expensive? I looked into it and was surprised to learn that vanilla beans actually come from orchids. I read a post written by the Spice House (where I occasionally order spices and vanilla beans from), which stated that the first harvest of the vanilla orchid vine doesn't happen for three years, taking eight years for maximum harvest. The flower blooms for only one or two days, which requires hand-pollination, and then it takes four to nine months after that for the vanilla pod to mature. They are then harvested and dried for several more months. When all that is considered, it's not surprising why they carry such a high price tag.

YIELD: 1 WECK pint

10 vanilla beans, halved
   lengthwise
2 cups 70-proof vodka,
   bourbon, or rum (no need for
   expensive brands, as the flavor
   will be overtaken by vanilla)

The most popular vanilla beans used for making homemade extract are Madagascar Bourbon, Tahitian, and Mexican. Each offers a bit of a different flavor, but all are delicious options. Mix and match if you'd like! There are different grades of vanilla beans and grade B are most used for extract making but feel free to use grade A if you have those on hand.

Slice the vanilla beans down the center lengthwise and add them to a clean WECK pint jar. Pour vodka over the vanilla beans, submerging them completely. Add the glass WECK jar lid and rubber ring to the rim of the jar and clip the metal clamps directly across from one another. Shake up the jar a little and store in a dark, room-temperature place as you'd keep any other liquor. Tip the jar upside down to mix up the vodka and vanilla beans occasionally. The vodka will slowly infuse with flavor from the beans and gain more and more flavor over time, and the vodka will begin to darken. It is ideal to wait 12 months before using, but taste test after 6 months and determine if the flavor is bold enough to use in baking and other cooking.

Once complete, you can remove the beans from the extract. If you don't want any vanilla beans present in the extract, you can strain them out with cheesecloth and a sieve or with a coffee filter. Store the extract in a pint WECK jar with lid, rubber ring, and clamps on securely, and it will keep wonderfully until you use it up. To reuse the beans, just repeat this method with the "used beans" and add in a few fresh beans (sliced lengthwise) and infuse for another year!

NOTES

ELDERBERRY SYRUP

This refrigerator recipe is made with honey instead of maple syrup (see page 55 for the water-bath canned version of this recipe). I keep this recipe out of the water bath because I don't want to heat the honey. Avoid if you have an allergy or hypersensitivity to elder or honeysuckle plants.

YIELD: 1 WECK quart jar (3 cups finished syrup)

½ cup dried organic elderberries (or 1 cup if using fresh/frozen elderberries)
4 cups water
1 cinnamon stick
1 tsp. ground ginger or 1-inch hunk of fresh ginger, peeled
1 cup raw honey
Vanilla extract or bean, or ½ tsp. whole cloves (optional, for different flavor outcomes)

In a medium pot, bring elderberries and water to a boil and then reduce to a medium-high simmer for 30 minutes. Remove from heat and allow the mixture to cool until lukewarm, then strain through a fine mesh sieve, reserving the liquid in a bowl or measuring cup. Use the back of a spoon to press down on the berries, to extract as much liquid as possible. Mix in the honey until dissolved, and transfer to a clean WECK quart jar. Clip the glass WECK lid with rubber ring in place. This syrup will last 6+ months refrigerated.

NOTES

FLAVORED SALTS

The flavor combinations you can create with this recipe are endless. Infused salts are a great way to add a pop of flavor when cooking, baking, and cocktail mixing. And as with most food preservation, they make a great, unique, and affordable gift! Feel free to add more of each ingredient if you want a more pronounced flavor.

YIELD: ¼ cup

¼ cup coarse kosher salt

SEASONING OPTIONS:

- I tsp. fresh citrus or fresh herbs
- I tsp. fresh ginger, finely grated
- I tsp. sriracha

In a small bowl, mix together salt with ingredient(s) of choice and stir well. Use a funnel to transfer salt mixture to the WECK jar. If using fresh/wet ingredients, allow salt mixture to sit with cover off jar overnight. The next day, stir again and place the WECK glass lid with rubber ring in place over the rim of the jar, and securely clip the jar shut with the two metal clamps, one directly across from the other.

Allow the salt mixture to infuse with flavors for a day or two; the flavor will intensify over a few days. Label and date jar. Store at room temperature, 60 to 75°F (15 to 23°C), out of direct sunlight, and use within 1 year. The infused flavors will weaken over time. You may notice the salt clumping together (depending on ingredients used). If this occurs, you can break it apart with a fork, mortar and pestle, or a seasoning grinder.

NOTES

ROASTED GARLIC SALT

Why spend several dollars on a jar of roasted garlic salt when you can make your own for a fraction of the price? It is so delicious, I use it on almost everything I cook.

YIELD: 1 WECK jam jar

1 small bulb of garlic
Drizzle of olive oil
½ cup coarse kosher salt

Preheat oven to 375°F. Slice off the top of 1 small bulb of garlic (7 to 9 small cloves). Drizzle olive oil over each clove, wrap bulb in foil, completely sealed, place in a glass pan or on a baking sheet, and bake for 40 minutes. Allow roasted garlic bulb to cool, remove roasted garlic from skin, and reserve in a small bowl. Smash garlic with fork, slowly add in the salt, and mix together with the roasted garlic. Once all the garlic and salt are thoroughly blended together, spread the garlic salt in an even layer on a parchment paper–lined baking sheet and bake at 165°F for 20 to 30 minutes, or until the salt is dry and flaky. Stir after 10 minutes. A food dehydrator can also be used for this final step if you prefer. Use fork or spatula to break up chunks of salt.

Use a funnel to transfer the salt mixture into a clean WECK jar. Place the WECK glass lid with rubber ring in place over the rim of the jar, and securely clip the jar shut with the two metal clamps, one directly across from the other. Label and date jar. Store at room temperature, 60 to 75°F (15 to 23°C), out of direct sunlight, and use within 1 year. If salt is clumped together, you can break it up by lightly blending it, or using a mortar and pestle to slightly break it down. For a finer finished salt, use a seasoning grinder. Note: If you use more garlic than noted in the recipe (or if the cloves are large), be prepared to bake the salt longer to dry it out. It will also clump together more in this case.

After making the garlic salt, consider stirring in other dried herbs and seasonings to alter the flavor such as dehydrated onions, dried oregano, dried basil, ground pepper, or dried chili flakes.

NOTES

FLAVORED SUGARS

The method of flavoring sugar is extremely similar to infusing salts. And as flavored salts, flavored sugars are also a great way to add a pop of flavor when cooking, baking, and cocktail mixing. With the addition of a little flavor, the sugar is completely transformed.

YIELD: 1 WECK Mini Mold jar, makes about ½ cup

½ cup organic or non-GMO granulated sugar

SEASONING OPTIONS:

- 1½ tsp. cinnamon
- 2½ tsp. espresso beans, finely ground
- Holiday spiced sugar (½ tsp. ground cinnamon, ½ tsp. ground clove, and ⅓ tsp. ground nutmeg)
- 1 vanilla bean, seeds removed from pod and stirred into sugar, include pod in jar
- 1½ tsp. citrus zest
- 1½ tsp. edible dried flowers
- 1½ tsp. dried herbs

To flavor sugar, in a small bowl, mix together sugar with ingredient(s) of choice and stir well. Use a funnel to transfer sugar mixture into WECK jar. If using fresh/wet ingredients, allow sugar mixture to sit with cover off jar overnight. The next day, stir again and place the WECK glass lid with rubber ring in place over the rim of the jar, and securely clip the jar shut with the two metal clamps, one directly across from the other.

Allow the sugar mixture to infuse with flavors; the flavor will intensify over a few days. Label and date jar. Store at room temperature, 60 to 75°F (15 to 23°C), out of direct sunlight, and use within 1 year. The infused flavors will weaken over time.

NOTES

INFUSED HONEY

Infused honey can be used for cooking, baking, stirring into teas, mixing into oatmeal or yogurt, or drizzling over a soft cheese on a crunchy baguette. The opportunities for use of infused honey are endless, and it is incredibly simple to make.

YIELD: 1 WECK jam jar (1 cup)

1 cup local mild honey (naturally flavorful honey will overpower the infused flavor)

1 tsp. dried herb(s) of choice such as cloves, cardamom pods, cinnamon, vanilla beans, chili peppers, star anise, coffee, ginger root, garlic, lavender flowers, rose petals (or other dried edible flower petals), peppermint leaves, thyme, rosemary, orange or lemon peel, or other dehydrated herbs

Add dried ingredients of choice to the bottom of a clean glass WECK jar. (It is not recommended to use fresh ingredients because the liquid contained in them could cause the honey to mold after several weeks unrefrigerated.) If using a vanilla bean, slice the pod down the middle, scrape out the seeds, add them to the jar, and include the pod as well (cut into pieces to fit). Pour honey over the dried ingredients, leaving ½ inch of headspace.

Once your infusion is ready, wipe the rim of the jar clean with a dampened lint-free cloth or paper towel. Place the glass WECK lid with rubber ring in place over the rim of the jar and carefully clip the two metal clamps on the jar directly across from one another.

Allow honey to infuse 7 or more days. The longer it infuses, the stronger the flavor. When the honey is flavored to your liking, use a fine mesh strainer and a measuring cup to strain out the solids. Store the infused honey in a WECK jar with the lid clamped on at room temperature, 60 to 75°F (15 to 23°C), out of direct sunlight.

NOTES

INFUSED MAPLE SYRUP

We have been tapping our maple trees and making homemade maple syrup for the last several years. Though pure maple syrup is perfect as is, we noticed infused maple syrup hitting the markets and decided to make our own—YUM! For these recipes, you do not need to make your own homemade syrup, but 100 percent pure maple syrup is recommended for best flavor as the base. You'll find that it is much more cost-effective to make your own infusions, and they also make fantastic gifts. Curious how to use infused maple syrup? Well, use it as you would any regular maple syrup (on pancakes, waffles, ice cream, oatmeal and yogurt), as well as for baking, in cocktails, drizzled over proteins, blended into a salad dressing, brushed onto salmon, or splashed over roasted veggies.

YIELD: 1 WECK jam jar (1 cup)

To make my favorite infusions, use any
    combination of these ingredients:

½ vanilla bean, slit down the center, seeds
    scraped out and pod included

2 cinnamon sticks for a light cinnamon
    flavor or 1 tbsp. ground cinnamon for a
    strong cinnamon flavor

2 tsp. whole coffee beans

1–2 dried hot peppers of choice

1 tsp. dried ginger, cardamom pods, or
    other dried herbs

2 tsp. dried fruits and berries

In a medium saucepan, heat one cup of maple syrup to a low simmer and add ingredient(s) of choice. I direct you to use a medium saucepan instead of a small saucepan because the syrup tends to boil over if heated for too long or allowed to get too hot. Simmer 5 minutes, then remove from heat and allow the syrup to cool slightly.

Transfer the infused syrup to a clean prepared WECK jar. You can leave the ingredients in the syrup or strain them out with a fine mesh strainer, the choice is yours. Once jarred, wipe the rim of the jar with a dampened, clean, lint-free cloth or paper towel and again with a dry towel. Place the glass WECK lid and rubber ring in place over the rim of the jar and carefully clip the two metal clamps on the jar directly across from one another. Once the syrup is completely cooled, transfer to the refrigerator. Use within 1 year.

NOTES

INFUSED VINEGARS

Use infused vinegars to enhance the flavor of your meals! Infuse a vinegar with just one or several of the items listed below. Be sure all fresh fruit and herbs are thoroughly washed and trimmed of any bruised or flawed areas before using.

YIELD: 1 WECK pint

Vinegar of choice (white wine vinegar and champagne vinegar are ideal for infusing as they have a gentle flavor compared to distilled white vinegar)

1 cup fresh fruit such as raspberries, strawberries, blackberries, cherries, blueberries, marionberry, huckleberries, skin of one orange, lemon, lime, or other citrus (no pith), pomegranate, peach, plum, red/black currant, or fig. Gently bruise fruit before adding to jar

3 tbsp. dried herbs such as oregano, tarragon, rosemary, basil, dill, sage, spicy peppers (crushed), cinnamon, lavender

3 sprigs fresh herbs such as oregano, tarragon, garlic clove, rosemary, mint, chives, chive blossoms, basil, dill, sage, fennel, spicy peppers (halved), or ginger

Cleanliness is imperative to a successful vinegar infusion. It is required that jars are sterilized before use. To sterilize jars, first wash all parts of the jar (lid and rubber ring as well) with warm soapy water, then boil the lid and bottle in a hot pot of water for ten minutes. Keep the jars warm until they are ready to fill with vinegar. Place the rubber rings in a small saucepan and heat them to a gentle simmer, then reduce heat and keep them warm until use.

In a small nonreactive saucepan, heat vinegar of choice up to 190 to 195°F, just before boiling point. Place fruit or herbs in a warm, prepared jar. Using a funnel, carefully ladle or pour the warm vinegar into the prepared jar, leaving ¼ inch of headspace. Wipe the rim of the jar with a dampened, clean, lint-free cloth or paper towel and again with a dry towel. Place the glass lid with rubber ring in place over the rim of the jar and carefully clip the two metal clamps on the jar directly across from one another. Once cooled completely, store in a dark cool place for 4 weeks as the flavors infuse.

Once the flavors have infused to your liking, transfer to the refrigerator for storage. If you want to remove the solids, use a fine mesh strainer to strain out the solids and rebottle them in a new, freshly sterilized jar. Label and date. Store in the refrigerator for best freshness and flavor. Use within 6 months.

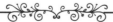

This method of infusing vinegar follows the rules and methods of the University of Georgia Cooperative Extension Service. They state that if any mold or yeast occurs, to throw out the vinegar. If any signs of fermentation occur (cloudiness, or sliminess), discard vinegar. Your hands, prep area, and supplies must be clean, as harmful bacteria can survive in some vinegars.

I love having pickled eggs on hand. They make a satisfying snack between meals, and pickling them with different ingredients gives the egg a completely different flavor outcome. Here are two of my most popular pickled egg recipes.

PICKLED EGGS

YIELD: 1 WECK pint jar

5–6 hard-boiled eggs, peeled
1 tbsp. pickling spices
1 tbsp. yellow onion, thinly sliced

BRINE:

1 cup white distilled vinegar (5 percent acidity)
1 tbsp. organic or non-GMO granulated sugar
1 tbsp. canning salt

Add eggs, pickling spices, and onion to a clean WECK pint jar. In a small nonreactive saucepan, prepare the brine. Bring the brine to a simmer and stir until the sugar and salt have dissolved. Remove from heat and cool slightly.

Using a funnel, carefully ladle or pour the brine over the eggs until they are completely submerged. Wipe the rim of the jar with a clean, dampened lint-free cloth or paper towel to remove any spillage. Place the glass WECK lid and rubber ring in place over the rim of the WECK jar and clamp the two metal clips securely on the jar directly across from one another.

Once the jar is no longer hot to the touch, transfer it to the refrigerator. Allow the eggs to pickle at least 1 week (if you can help yourself), but ideally 2 weeks before eating. The longer they pickle, the more flavor they will have. Eat eggs within 4 months for best flavor and texture.

NOTES

SPICY PICKLED EGGS

YIELD: 1 WECK quart jar

10–12 hard-boiled eggs, peeled
1–2 jalapeños, halved
2 garlic cloves, chopped
2 tsp. red pepper flakes
4 sprigs fresh dill

BRINE:

1 cup water
1 cup white distilled vinegar (5 percent acidity)
1 tbsp. canning salt

Add all ingredients to a clean WECK quart jar, wedging the jalapeño slices between the eggs. In a small nonreactive saucepan, prepare the brine. Bring the brine to a simmer and stir until the salt has dissolved. Remove from heat and cool slightly.

Using a funnel, carefully ladle or pour the brine over the eggs until they are completely submerged. Wipe the rim of the jar with a clean, dampened lint-free cloth or paper towel to remove any spillage. Place the glass WECK lid and rubber ring in place over the rim of the WECK jar and clamp the two metal clips securely on the jar directly across from one another.

Once the jar is no longer hot to the touch, transfer it to the refrigerator. Allow the eggs to pickle for at least 1 week (if you can help yourself), but ideally 2 weeks before eating. The longer they pickle, the more flavor they will have. Eat eggs within 4 months for best flavor and texture.

NOTES

PICKLED GINGER

This recipe is contributed by my friend, LaRae Burk, canning editor at @thefeedfeed and owner of the blog chezlarae.com. LaRae says "Skip the red dye and corn syrup that you find in store-bought pickled ginger and make your own at home. Use the freshest ginger available to you, preferably with a shiny exterior. The skin should be thin; not gnarly and thick. Serve with sushi, poke bowls, scrambled eggs, grilled salmon, or tofu soup."

YIELD: 1 WECK pint

8 ounces fresh ginger

BRINE:

1 cup rice vinegar
¾ cup organic or non-GMO granulated
  sugar
½ cup water
1 ½ tsp. kosher salt

Wash and peel ginger, using a spoon to gently scrape off the skin, or vegetable peeler if preferred. Slice into paper-thin strips using a paring knife or ideally a mandolin slicer if you have one available to you. Pack the ginger strips into a clean WECK pint jar.

In a small nonreactive saucepan, bring the brine ingredients to a boil. Once the sugar has dissolved, using a funnel, carefully ladle or pour the brine over the sliced ginger until the ginger slices are completely submerged. Wipe the rim of the jar with a clean, dampened lint-free cloth or paper towel to remove any spillage. Place the glass WECK lid and rubber ring in place over the rim of the jar and clamp the two metal clips securely on the jar directly across from one another.

Once the jar is no longer hot to the touch, transfer it to the refrigerator. Allow the ginger to pickle for at least 2 hours, or ideally up to 2 days before eating. The longer they pickle, the more flavor they will have. Eat within 2 months.

NOTES

PRESERVED LEMONS

There are different methods for preserving lemons, but this is my no-fail go-to process of choice. It is convenient to have preserved lemons at my fingertips for cooking with year-round. I toss them into simmer sauces and include them in the water when I poach eggs, shrimp, and other seafood. And they are great to use in homemade vinaigrettes.

YIELD: 1 WECK quart jar

3–4 (or more depending on size) fresh
   organic lemons
3–4 tbsp. kosher salt

Scrub lemons clean. Unless you are certain that the lemons you are using are free of food-grade wax, it is worth taking the next step to remove any wax that may be present on the fruit. To do so, put the lemons in a colander in the sink, and carefully pour boiling water over them.

Trim off ends of lemons and cut them into quarters lengthwise. Discard seeds as they fall out, but no need to remove all. In a clean WECK jar, sprinkle some salt on the bottom of the jar, and pack in one layer of lemons. Repeat the salting and layering method until the jar is full. Push and gently smash the lemons as you fill the jar so that some of the lemon juice releases and there is no space between the lemon slices, leaving ½ inch of headspace. Once the jar is tightly packed, sprinkle the remaining salt over the lemon slices. Through the process, enough lemon juice should have naturally been created to cover the lemon slices. If not, juice another lemon and pour the juice over the jarred lemon slices until they are completely submerged. Use a lid from a smaller WECK jar as a weight to push down the lemon slices under the lemon juice. Wipe the rim of the jar with a dampened lint-free towel or paper towel. Add the glass WECK lid with rubber ring onto the rim of the jar and clip it securely closed with the two metal clamps, one directly across from the other. Store at room temperature, 60 to 75°F (15 to 23°C), out of direct sunlight. The lemons will stay preserved as long as they are submerged under the salt-juice brine.

To use, remove the lemon slices from the jar, remove seeds, and you can either rinse them off before use, or if looking to add saltiness, use them as-is. For example, if I'm poaching shrimp, I leave the salt on because I don't mind the salted water, but generally the salt will be rinsed off. I use the whole quarter wedge when simmering in water, though the pulp is ideal for simmering in sauces and the chopped peel is ideal for using uncooked in dishes, such as salads.

To flavor the preserved lemons, consider adding one of these (or a combination of these) ingredients: one cinnamon stick, 2 bay leaves, 1 tsp. dried cloves, allspice berries, dried oregano, chili peppers, cardamom, or whole black peppercorns.

MEYER LEMON AND ALMOND CURD

This recipe has been contributed by my friend, Pam Lillis, a Master Preserver and Certified Nutritional Health Coach based in Connecticut. Pam says "The faint pairing of almond makes this curd perfect for scones, tarts, and is great as a dip for fruit or your favorite shortbread cookies." Additional tools for this recipe include a double boiler, hand citrus juicer, whisk, fine mesh strainer, spatula, and grater/zester.

YIELD: **3 WECK jam jars (3 cups)**

1 ½ cups fresh Meyer or other variety lemon juice + zest

2 large eggs

4 egg yolks, whites removed

¾ cup superfine cane sugar or granulated sugar that has been run through a grinder/blender

¼ tsp. fine sea salt (optional)

1 ½ sticks (¾ cup) unsalted butter, chilled and cubed

1 ½ tsp. natural almond extract

Scrub lemons clean. Unless you are certain that the lemons you are using are free of food-grade wax, it is worth taking the next step to remove any wax that may be present on the fruit. To do so, put the lemons in a colander in the sink, and carefully pour boiling water over them. Zest two lemons and set aside. Juice lemons until you have 1 ½ cups of fresh lemon juice; pulp is fine to include. Try to remove seeds as you are able, though they will be strained out at the end. Reserve lemon zest.

Heat water in the double boiler to a medium simmer (you do not want a rolling boil). If you do not have a metal pan double boiler set up, you can use a medium saucepan and a heat-tolerant glass or metal bowl. Do not allow the water to touch the bottom of the bowl, as it will heat the curd too much.

In a nonreactive bowl, whisk together the eggs and gradually add lemon juice and zest, sugar, and salt (optional). Transfer the mixture to the top of the double boiler (or over the simmering pot), and begin to add in the cubed butter, one at a time. Add almond extract. Whisk constantly as the butter melts and the curd starts to thicken; this could take 15 minutes or more.

Once it begins to thicken, dip a spatula or wooden spoon into the curd to test it. The curd should coat the surface of the utensil. Once thickened to satisfaction, remove from heat. Place the fine mesh strainer over a glass measuring cup or bowl and pour the curd through the strainer to ensure a smooth consistency.

Transfer the lemon curd to clean WECK jars, add the rubber ring and glass lid and clamp shut. Store in the refrigerator for up to 2 weeks, or freeze for up to 1 year with a WECK "Keep-Fresh Cover."

NOTES

NOTES

SPROUTS GROWN IN A WECK® JAR

Growing sprouts at home is incredibly simple and very inexpensive. They are tasty, nutritious, and add a delightful crunch to a sandwich, salad, taco, soup, or just eaten as is. The most common sprout that we grow at home is alfalfa, though this sprouting method will work for all sorts of sprouting seeds such as clover, mustard, radish, and broccoli (though broccoli will likely take 2 days longer to sprout than the others). My mom has been sprouting seeds for decades and this is the no-fail method she taught me years ago.

YIELD: I WECK quart jar

I tbsp. organic sprouting seeds (alfalfa, clover, mustard, radish or a mixture of all)
Water, as needed
Cheesecloth, cut large enough to cover the top of the jar
I rubber binder
Patience, about 5–6 days' worth

Add I tbsp. seeds into a clean WECK quart jar, fill with cool water until the seeds are submerged, and add about 1 to 2 inches of water. Cover jar with cheesecloth and secure it with a rubber binder. Soak overnight.

After the seeds have soaked 12+ hours, pour out the water and rinse the seeds once more and drain. Cover the top of the jar with cheesecloth once again, and secure with the rubber binder. Turn the jar horizontally and slowly rotate the jar to spread the seeds out so that some will stick to the sides of the jar. Store in a dark place out of direct sunlight, at room temperature, 60 to 75°F (15 to 23°C). Store the jar horizontally on its side. You want to avoid the seeds piling in a wet mass in the jar, or they may mold. Repeat the steps of rinsing the seeds daily until the sprouts have grown I to 2 inches. It takes about 5 to 6 days until they are ready to eat, or 6 to 7 days for broccoli.

Once the sprouts have grown enough to eat, take the amount you want from the jar and continue to rinse daily for a couple of days and allow them to continue to grow on the counter as you use them. If longer-term storage is needed, give them a final rinse and drain well. Place sprouts in a sunny window briefly, for 20 minutes or less, to allow them to turn a vibrant green. Add the glass WECK lid with rubber ring and securely clamp on the lid with the two metal clamps directly across from one another. Transfer to the refrigerator and eat within I week.

PART III

BLANCHING TIMES FOR VEGETABLES

VEGETABLE	TIME* in minutes
Asparagus, medium	2
Beans, green and wax	3
Beans, lima and pinto	3
Broccoli florets	3
Brussels sprouts	4
Cabbage, shredded	1½
Carrots, sliced	2
Cauliflower, florets	3
Corn	5–6
Eggplant	4
Kohlrabi, cubed	1
Okra, medium	3
Peas, edible pod	2
Potatoes	3–5
Summer Squash	3
Turnips, cubed	2

*Blanching times given are for boiling-water blanching method. Double the time if using a steam method for blanching.

FREEZING WITH WECK®

WECK jars are great for freezing fruits and vegetables! The jars keep an airtight seal, which defers freezer burn. It is recommended to use the style of jars with the straight sides (mold-style), with wide mouth openings. WECK also offers "Keep Fresh" lids, which they recommend for freezing foods. Please remember that food expands when it is frozen, so it is important to leave proper headspace to avoid breakage. It is also necessary to avoid extreme changes in temperature, so be sure that all hot foods are completely cooled before freezing. Here are some tips for freezing fruits and vegetables, provided by WECK:

Freezing Fruits

Syrup Pack: Dissolve 1 part sugar in 2 parts water, then chill. Pack fruit into jars and pour syrup over fruit. Leave ½ inch of headspace for ¼ liter (1 cup) and ½ liter (2 cups = pint) jars and 1 inch of headspace for 1-liter (4 cups = quart) jars. Clip shut jar with rubber ring, lid, and clamps or add "Keep Fresh" lid.

Sugar Pack: Coat fruit pieces with sugar, then pack into jars using ½ inch of headspace. Clip jar shut with rubber ring, lid, and clamps or add "Keep Fresh" lid.

Tray Pack, a.k.a. "IQF: Individually Quick Frozen": Freeze fruit on a tray for 1 hour, then pack into jars. Very little headspace is needed in this case, as the fruit is already frozen. Clip jar shut with rubber ring, lid, and clamps or add "Keep Fresh" lid.

Freezing Vegetables

- Wash and strain vegetables before removing skins or hulls. Cut into pieces if necessary.
- Blanch vegetables before freezing to inactivate enzymes. Use 1 gallon of water for 1 lb. of vegetables. Follow times in blanching chart (pg. 146).
- Chill vegetables in ice water for same time as blanching time, then drain or allow to dry on lint-free towels.

Packing Vegetables

Dry Pack: Pack vegetables into jars leaving ½ inch of headspace. Clip jar shut with rubber ring, lid, and clamps or add "Keep Fresh" lid.

Tray Pack (IQF): Freeze vegetable pieces for 1 hour, then pack into jars. Very little headspace is needed since the vegetables are already frozen. Clip shut jar with rubber ring, lid, and clamps or add "Keep Fresh" lid.

TROUBLESHOOTING

A water-bath canned jar did not seal or unsealed after storage.

Very rarely will a jar not seal. This is likely due to a faulty rubber ring or a defect in the rim of the jar. Perhaps there was a chip or crack that was not noticed before processing.

If a jar becomes unsealed after processing, chances are that the preserve was not properly processed. If the water bath did not reach a boil for 10 minutes or more—time varies per recipe—the bacteria in the canned food may not have been killed, therefore the gases within the preserve will have pushed the lid off the sealed jar. This is meant as a safety warning for you to detect preserves that are unsafe to eat. All contents should be discarded if this occurs.

Other signs that a canned good has spoiled: foul odor, slime, mold, or bubbling (fermentation). Like my grandpa always says, "When in doubt, throw it out!"

The fermented food is cloudy.

The brine of a ferment will become cloudy; this is part of the process of fermentation and an indication that things are going exactly as they should. You may even notice sediment on the vegetable or at the bottom of the jar.

My ferment is moldy.

It is crucial that you keep all veggies underneath the brine to keep them safe from the air. If a piece of cabbage is poking out of the brine, it is susceptible to mold. That is why I recommend checking on the ferments daily to make sure everything is looking and smelling good, that all the veggies are under the brine, and that there is no sign of kahm yeast or mold.

My fermenting jars are overflowing.

It is totally normal for a very active ferment to overflow a bit. This can be curbed by leaving proper headspace, "burping" your ferment daily to release any gas buildup, and pushing the produce back down if it has risen due to carbon dioxide buildup. If a ferment seems more active than others, burp it 2 to 3 times a day. You can also put the jar in a bowl or tray to catch any overflow instead of making a fer-*mess*. Otherwise, remove some of the fermenting produce and add it to another jar so each jar can have 1 to 2 inches of headspace, as needed.

Why did the garlic turn green?

Occasionally garlic turns green or blue during fermentation and canning. This is nothing to worry about; it's a natural chemical reaction that can occur.

OTHER USES FOR WECK® JARS

- Candle holder
- Craft storage (beads, decorative tapes, beads, scrapbooking supplies, etc.)
- Dehydrated food storage
- Dessert dishware
- Drinking glasses
- Flower vase
- Homemade bath salts or sugar scrubs
- Homemade lotion or candle storage
- Homemade terraria
- Leftover food storage
- Lids can be used as a tea-light holder
- Pantry organization for dried foods
- One-serving desserts
- Salad to go
- Salt or seasoning storage jars
- Yogurt parfait to go

RESOURCES

The J. WECK Company: weckjars.com

Shop online for a complete selection of WECK jars, replacement lids, rubber rings, metal clasps, and other WECK home preservation supplies.

WECK Jar Suppliers:

Amazon.com
Container Store: containerstore.com
Cost Plus World Market
Crate & Barrel: crateandbarrel.com
Food52.com
Heath Ceramics: heathceramics.com
School House Electric & Supply Co.: schoolhouse.com
Terrain: shopterrain.com
The Container Store: containerstore.com
Williams Sonoma: williams-sonoma.com
World Market: worldmarket.com

Canning Crafts Labels: canningcrafts.com

Gorgeous jar labels and tags, completely customizable.

National Center for Home Preservation: http://nchfp.uga.edu

A wonderful resource of research-based recommendations for most methods of home food preservation.

NW Ferments: nwferments.com

A great resource for fermentation supplies such as starter cultures for home production, as well as airlocks, salt, and more.

Stone Creek Trading: stonecreektrading.com

A great resource for fermentation-related supplies such as crocks, weights, cabbage shredders, cabbage pounders, and more.

Wild Fermentation: wildfermentation.com

Sandor Katz's website includes links to his books, which go in depth about the process and history of fermentation, as well as recipes for fermented vegetables, cheese, yogurt, bread, and more.

The Spice House: www.thespicehouse.com

Great variety of organic spices in bulk.

ABOUT THE AUTHOR

Stephanie Thurow first learned the kitchen craft of water-bath canning in the early 2000s. What initially started as a mission to make the perfect garlic dill pickle quickly morphed into a way of life. She finds great pride in canning and fermenting fresh organic produce that can be preserved for year-round enjoyment and shared with her loved ones. She enjoys teaching others how to cook and preserve from scratch and wants to empower people to try their hand at preserving from the comfort of their homes. Her nonintimidating approach to home preservation puts even a novice at ease. Stephanie is a Certified Master Food Preserver and food preservation instructor.

Stephanie's first cookbook, *Can It & Ferment It* (2017), brings the canning and fermenting communities together by offering recipes that work for both canning and fermenting. Readers will learn how to preserve each fruit and vegetable featured in the cookbook with two different methods; each can be enjoyed water-bath canned or as a healthy, probiotic-rich ferment. Recipes are organized by season. #canitandfermentit

Stephanie's second cookbook, *WECK Small-Batch Preserving* (2018) is the first collaboration cookbook with WECK Jar Company. Thurow created a step-by-step guide to using the versatile, all-glass WECK jars for water-bath canning, fermenting, freezing, infusing, and more.

Connect with Stephanie

Minnesota from Scratch Blog: www.minnesotafromscratch.com
Instagram: @minnesotafromscratch
Twitter: @StephLovestoCan
Facebook: facebook.com/MinnesotaFromScratch/
YouTube: Stephanie Thurow
Use hashtags: #canitandfermentit #wecksmallbatch #weckhomepreserving

ACKNOWLEDGMENTS

Thank you to my editor, Nicole Mele, and my publisher Skyhorse Publishing, for proposing such a fantastic collaboration. I'm pleased to have the opportunity to write a second food preservation guide for the WECK Company. I'm honored to be chosen to represent these gorgeous, eco-friendly, and versatile jars.

Kindest regards to all my friends and family who are always enthusiastic about taste testing my experimental creations and offering invaluable feedback. I appreciate your support.

Thank you to my gracious contributors, who each shared a delicious recipe for this book: Sue Ross Depaolo, Wendy Jensen, Pam Lillis, and LaRae Burk.

Finally, thank you to my husband and daughter, who are the best supporters, helpers, and teammates I could ever wish for. I appreciate you both more than you could ever imagine.

NOTES

NOTES

NOTES

CONVERSION CHARTS

METRIC AND IMPERIAL CONVERSIONS
(These conversions are rounded for convenience)

Ingredient	Cups/Tablespoons/ Teaspoons	Ounces	Grams/Milliliters
Butter	1 cup = 16 tablespoons = 2 sticks	8 ounces	230 grams
Cheese, shredded	1 cup	4 ounces	110 grams
Cream cheese	1 tablespoon	0.5 ounce	14.5 grams
Cornstarch	1 tablespoon	0.3 ounce	8 grams
Flour, all-purpose	1 cup/1 tablespoon	4.5 ounces/0.3 ounce	125 grams/8 grams
Flour, whole wheat	1 cup	4 ounces	120 grams
Fruit, dried	1 cup	4 ounces	120 grams
Fruits or veggies, chopped	1 cup	5 to 7 ounces	145 to 200 grams
Fruits or veggies, pureed	1 cup	8.5 ounces	245 grams
Honey, maple syrup, or corn syrup	1 tablespoon	0.75 ounce	20 grams
Liquids: cream, milk, water, or juice	1 cup	8 fluid ounces	240 milliliters
Oats	1 cup	5.5 ounces	150 grams
Salt	1 teaspoon	0.2 ounce	6 grams
Spices: cinnamon, cloves, ginger, or nutmeg (ground)	1 teaspoon	0.2 ounce	5 milliliters
Sugar, brown, firmly packed	1 cup	7 ounces	200 grams
Sugar, white	1 cup/1 tablespoon	7 ounces/0.5 ounce	200 grams/12.5 grams
Vanilla extract	1 teaspoon	0.2 ounce	4 grams

OVEN TEMPERATURES

Fahrenheit	Celsius	Gas Mark
225°	110°	¼
250°	120°	½
275°	140°	1
300°	150°	2
325°	160°	3
350°	180°	4
375°	190°	5
400°	200°	6
425°	220°	7
450°	230°	8

INDEX